Rethinking
Realized Eschatology

I distinguish between exegesis of particular passages and interpretation in the wider sense.
—*C. H. Dodd*

When all evidence in the sayings of Jesus for "realized eschatology" is thoroughly tested, it boils down to ἔφθασεν ἐφ' ὑμᾶς of Matthew 12:28 and Luke 11:20. Why should that determine the interpretation of Matthew 6:10 and Luke 11:2? Why should a difficult, obscure saying establish the meaning of one that is clear and unambiguous?
—*Millar Burrows*

Rethinking
Realized Eschatology

• *Clayton Sullivan* •

MERCER

PEETERS

ISBN 0-86554-302-X

Rethinking Realized Eschatology
Copyright © 1988
Mercer University Press
All rights reserved
Printed in the United States of America

The paper used in this publication meets
the minimum requirements of American National Standard
for Information Sciences—Permanence of Paper
for Printed Library Materials, ANSI Z39.48–1984.

Library of Congress Cataloging-in-Publication Data
Sullivan, Clayton, 1930–
 Rethinking realized eschatolgy / Clayton Sullivan.
 ix + 144 pages ; 6x9 in. (15.25x23.85 cm.)
 Includes bibliographical references and index.
 ISBN 0-86554-302-X (alk. paper)
 1. Realized eschatology—Controversial literature.
2. Dodd, Charles Howard, 1884–1973. The parables of the kingdom. 3. Jesus Christ—Parables. 4. Kingdom of God—Biblical teaching. 5. Eschatology—Biblical teaching. 6. Bible. N.T. Gospels—Criticism, interpretation, etc. 7. Two-source hypothesis (Synoptic criticism)—controversial literature. I. Title.
BT819.5.S94   1988   88-6612
236—dc19   CIP

Contents

PREFACE vii

CHAPTER 1
An Introduction 1

CHAPTER 2
A Critique of Dodd's Utilization
of the Two-Document Hypothesis
in *The Parables of the Kingdom* 13

CHAPTER 3
A Comparison of the Use of *Basileia*
in the Writings of Dodd
and in the Synoptic Gospels 37

CHAPTER 4
The Kingdom Version of Realized Eschatology 65

CHAPTER 5
The Christological Version of Realized Eschatology 101

CHAPTER 6
Conclusion 113

APPENDIX I
A Listing of All References
to Kingdom in the Synoptic Gospels 119

APPENDIX II
The Kingdom of God in Patristic Literature 127

BIBLIOGRAPHY 141

INDEXES 147

To Mae and Charlotte

Preface

Students of Christian origins are of one mind in contending that the Kingdom of God was central in Jesus' teaching. Curiously enough, however, scholars have never been able to agree on what Jesus meant by this expression. Across the years the phrase "Kingdom of God" has been semantic putty—pulled, shaped, and squeezed in all directions. Some have interpreted the Kingdom in terms of first-century Judaism. Others "have internalized, de-temporalized, cosmologized, spiritualized, allegorized, mysticized, psychologized, philosophized, and sociologized the concept of the kingdom of God,"[1] attempting to make it viable for Christian theology. In short, interpreting the Kingdom of God has been a continuing hermeneutical Donnybrook Fair.

For the past half-century many Anglo-American exegetes have been devotees of *realized eschatology,* an exegetical-theological position associated with the late C. H. Dodd. This position contends the Kingdom was realized in Jesus' ministry. Like "form criticism" or the "Two-Document Hypothesis," realized eschatology has become a technical expression in New Testament studies. This book seeks to examine realized eschatology's cogency.

I am not unaware that some readers will view any critique—or questioning—of realized eschatology as a waste of time. Realized eschatology is now virtually an assumption in Anglo-American New Testament studies. Moreover, biblical scholarship has moved on to other issues, and the name of C. H. Dodd no longer suggests the cutting edge of biblical scholarship. Although Professor Dodd may be for some a remote figure, he nonetheless left his fingerprints on New Testament studies. He is as responsible as anyone for the centrality in contemporary hermeneutics of the assertion "If I by the spirit of God cast out the demons, then the Kingdom

---

[1] George Wesley Buchanan, *The Consequences of the Covenant* (Leiden: E. J. Brill, 1970) 55.

of God has come upon you" (Matthew 12:28 || Luke 11:20). For numerous exegetes this verse has become the interpretive cornerstone, the starting place, for understanding what Jesus meant by the Kingdom. Indeed, this assertion (Matthew 12:28 || Luke 11:20) is to present-day theologians what "The Kingdom of God is within you" (Luke 17:21) was to liberal theologians of two or three generations ago. The placing of Matthew 12:28 || Luke 11:20 as an interpretive cornerstone is an unfortunate development in New Testament studies. This untoward development will be dealt with in the course of this critique.

This study also brings into focus the insight that two "versions" of realized eschatology appear in C. H. Dodd's writings. In *The Parables of the Kingdom,* published in 1935 (revised edition, 1961), Professor Dodd advanced a "Kingdom version" of realized eschatology. This version contends the Kingdom of God was actualized in Jesus' career. In works published after 1935 Professor Dodd advanced a "Christological version" of realized eschatology. This version, patterned after R. G. Collingwood's philosophy of history, contends that the Christ event possesses ultimate religious meaning (significance). These two versions are not the same. Unfortunately, they are fused or intermingled in the minds of many Anglo-American New Testament scholars.

This book had its conception during my graduate studies in Greek New Testament at the Southern Baptist Theological Seminary in Louisville, Kentucky. While a graduate student during the 1960s, I came to have reservations about the Two-Document (or Two-Source) Hypothesis—particularly with regard to "Q" (the so-called "Sayings" source, a supposed compilation of the sayings of Jesus). I did not trust these reservations, however, for during the 1960s the Two-Document Hypothesis was an unquestioned dogma in New Testament studies. Fortunately, such is no longer the case, and in this book I attempt to reevaluate realized eschatology in the light of the current erosion of confidence in the Two-Document Hypothesis.[2] Indeed, a major task confronting New Testament students is a rethinking of theological structures that are based on the Two-Document Hypothesis. This book, I hope, will contribute to that task.

I express gratitude to Joan Williams, Eunice McSwain, Dr. Betty Drake, Dr. Stanley Hauer, and Dr. Michael DeArmey for their kind and able assistance in preparing this book for publication.

---

[2]A growing number of New Testament scholars are recognizing that "the priority of Mark [or the Two-Document Hypothesis] is *assuredly not* one of the assured results of New Testament scholarship" (so R. V. G. Tasker in conversation with C. S. Mann as reported by Mann in his *Mark: A New Translation with Introduction and Commentary,* Anchor Bible 27 [Garden City NY: Doubleday, 1986] viii; italics added).

CHAPTER
• 1 •

An Introduction

Flowing from Jesus of Nazareth, the Christian religion has been in existence for some two thousand years. Throughout most of this two-millenia span, the Church paid scant attention to Jesus as a Jew who lived at a specific time and place and who experienced life within a particular historical-cultural context. Instead, primary attention was given to doctrines or dogmas *about* Jesus. To express this matter another way, Christians have tended across the years to view Jesus through theological, not through historical, spectacles. Thus theologians have expended mental-speculative energy hammering out the Trinitarian Dogma. They have pondered: What significance did Jesus' death possess? How did both a divine and human nature coexist within him? This dogmatic approach explains why many Christians have conceived of Jesus not as a rabbi who once lived on the eastern fringe of the Roman empire, but as an "otherworldly" figure who has always resided in stained glass cathedral windows.

Yet two hundred years ago—approximately—a mutation took place in Christian thought, a mutation that was a by-product of the Enlightenment. Instead of further elaborating the Jesus of dogma, Christian thinkers began a quest for the historical Jesus—the human Jesus of flesh and blood who was a prophet in Galilee and was crucified by Pilate. This search for the historical Jesus was begun by Herman Samuel Reimarus, an obscure German scholar who was a professor of oriental languages in Hamburg and who died in 1768. His studies were posthumously published by G. E. Lessing—a librarian, philosopher, and theologian—in a collection entitled the *Wolfenbüttel Fragments*. One of Reimarus's essays in this anthology was "On the Intentions of Jesus and His Disciples." The publication of this work in 1778, slightly more than two hundred years ago, marks the beginning of the "quest for the historical Jesus." Before Reimarus, no one had attempted to formulate a historical understanding of Jesus' life. Reimarus, by contrast, treated the gospels as historical documents and endeavored to place the events and ideas recorded in them in a historical context. Subsequently other scholars walked in Reimarus's footsteps. Indeed, throughout the nineteenth century scores of lives of Jesus were written by Christian scholars who grappled with such questions as: What was the historical, geographical, and ideological setting of Jesus' life? What message did Jesus proclaim to his contemporaries? What was his intention? What did he attempt to accomplish? What happened to him?

Out of this prolonged, intensive search for the historical Jesus an incontrovertible conclusion emerged: Jesus announced to the first-century Jewish world the imminent coming of the Kingdom of God. "Repent! The Kingdom of God is at hand!" John Reumann was on target in observing, "Ask any hundred New Testament scholars around the world, Protestant, Catholic, or non-Christian, what the central message of Jesus of Nazareth was, and the vast majority of them—perhaps every single expert—would agree that this message centered in the Kingdom of God."[1]

Curiously enough, however, students of Jesus' thought have never agreed among themselves on what is meant by the phrase "Kingdom of God." Some identified the Kingdom with the Church. Others equated it with a blessed future life. Still others suggested that the Kingdom was God's rule in human hearts or in society. This hermeneutical debate concerning the meaning of the Kingdom of God continued across the nineteenth century; it continued in an inconclusive manner, as though a casual discussion among ideological gourmets concerning noetic canapés. But this casual debate was interrupted in 1892 with the publication in Germany of Johannes Weiss's *Jesus' Proclamation of the Kingdom of God*.[2] This small book had a profound impact upon life-of-Jesus research. Weiss, resurrecting Reimarus, argued that Jesus' pronouncements concerning the Kingdom of God should be interpreted against a background of Jewish apocalyptic-eschatological expectations. Among Jesus' contemporaries, we now know,

---

[1] John Reumann, *Jesus in the Church's Gospels: Modern Scholarship and the Earliest Sources* (Philadelphia: Fortress Press, 1968) 142.

[2] The German title of Johannes Weiss's book was *Die Predigt Jesu vom Reiche Gottes*. In 1971 the English translation by Richard Hyde Hiers and David Larrimore Holland was published by Fortress Press (Philadelphia).

were Jews who believed the historical process was reaching its denouement. Something dramatic or cataclysmic was about to take place: the God of Israel was on the verge of intervening in human affairs in order to abolish injustice and to make things right on earth. Jesus, sharing these eschatological hopes, proclaimed the imminent coming of God's Kingdom to earth, a realm that was to be a golden age for repentant Jews. In New Testament studies this view that Jesus expected the imminent arrival of God's Kingdom on earth is known as "consistent eschatology." Consistent eschatology has been advocated by scholars as diverse as Albert Schweitzer, Martin Dibelius, Alfred Loisy, Charles Guignebert, Morton Scott Enslin, and Krister Stendahl. It currently dominates theological schools in Europe. For many, Rudolf Bultmann's observation of thirty years ago still holds true: "Today nobody doubts that Jesus' conception of the Kingdom of God is an eschatological one—at least in European theology."[3]

This eschatological view, however, was unwelcome to many Christian apologists. It was unwelcome because scholars such as Schweitzer and Loisy concluded that Jesus was mistaken in his prophecy. Jesus and his disciples believed and proclaimed that the Kingdom of God was about to appear on earth. Yet this expected Kingdom, so Schweitzer and his followers contend, *did not come*. As Martin Dibelius of the University of Heidelberg expressed the matter in his *Jesus* (1939): "It still looks as though a monstrous illusion lies at the basis of the whole mission of Jesus, the illusion of something immediately impending which actually never has come to pass."[4]

This conception of Jesus as a mistaken prophet, in error about the major theme of his preaching ministry, was contrary to the Church's dogmatic understanding of him as an infallible teacher. Moreover, Christian thinkers had always assumed a continuity between Jesus' message and the Church's message. "The Church teaches what Jesus taught." Yet if Jesus was mistaken, then the Kingdom concept was not only an embarrassment for Christian apologetics but a useless category for Christian theology.[5]

---

[3]Rudolf Bultmann, *Jesus Christ and Mythology* (New York: Charles Scribner's Sons, 1958) 13.

[4]Martin Dibelius, *Jesus* (Berlin: Walter de Gruyter, 1939), trans. Charles B. Hedrick and Frederick C. Grant (Philadelphia: Westminster Press, 1949) 70.

[5]Rudolf Bultmann quotes Julius Kaftan, his teacher in dogmatics in Berlin, as saying,

Throughout the opening decades of the twentieth century, an impasse existed in life-of-Jesus research. Consistent eschatology was an indigestible lump in the stew of New Testament studies. On the one hand, Weiss's and Schweitzer's view of Jesus as a mistaken prophet could not be neatly disproven; on the other hand, this view could not be glibly accepted. Consistent eschatology was like a renegade relative in attendance at a family reunion; its presence could be neither applauded nor denied.

In the context of this impasse a book was published in England in 1935 bearing the innocent title *The Parables of the Kingdom*.[6] Its author was the late C. H. Dodd, professor of New Testament studies at Cambridge University. Having less than two hundred pages, *The Parables of the Kingdom* turned out to be one of the most influential books ever published in New Testament studies. In this work Professor Dodd advanced a hypothesis known as *realized eschatology,* a phrase that has become embedded in the vocabulary of New Testament studies.[7] This hypothesis, contra Schweitzer, contended that the Kingdom of God was *realized* —or actualized—*in Jesus' ministry.* This thesis was not original with Professor Dodd; it had been expressed in 1909 by Henry Burton Sharman in his book *The Teach-*

"If Johannes Weiss is right and the conception of the Kingdom of God is an eschatological one, then it is impossible to make use of this conception in dogmatics" (see *Jesus Christ and Mythology,* 13).

[6]*The Parables of the Kingdom* was published in 1935 by James Nisbet and Company (London). In response to early critical discussion, a second edition appeared in March 1936 and a third edition in November 1936. A fourth edition was published in 1948, and the current "revised edition" was published in 1961 (American edition, New York: Charles Scribner's Sons). While the 1961 revised edition was "revised . . . throughout" the revisions consisted of only "minor changes and additions" and an update of references to recent works. References in the present work to *The Parables of the Kingdom* are by and large to the first edition (1935) or the third edition (1936) which includes Dodd's response (in the preface and some notes) to early criticism of the first edition.

[7]Although *The Parables of the Kingdom* was the first book in which Dodd published in full his view that the Kingdom of God was an abstract power actualized in Jesus, prolepses of this view can be seen in the following articles written by him prior to 1935: "The Eschatological Element in the New Testament and Its Permanent Significance," *The Interpreter* 20 (October 1923): 17-21; "The This-Worldly Kingdom of God in Our Lord's Teaching," *Theology* 14 (May 1927): 259; "Jesus as Teacher and Prophet," *Mysterium Christi,* ed. Bell and Deissmann (London: Longmans, 1930) 60ff.; "Miracles in the Gospels," *The Expository Times* 44 (August 1933): 505-506; "God in Christ," *The Expository Times* 46 (December 1934): 116-17.

*ing of Jesus about the Future.*⁸ The biblical evidence upon which Sharman based his contention was the same evidence used years later by Professor Dodd (Matthew 12:28; Luke 17:21; 16:16). In 1918 a similar view was expressed by William Manson in his Bruce Lectures published under the title *Christ's View of the Kingdom of God.*⁹ Parenthetically, the familiar phrase "realized eschatology" was anticipated by Manson when he observed that "The Gospel of Jesus, by presenting the Kingdom as something already cast like a seed into the ground, breaks through the moulds of apocalyptic thought, and diffuses itself in the world as a religion of *realized redemption.*"¹⁰ Likewise, a similarity exists between the thesis of *The Parables of the Kingdom* and ideas expressed by Rudolf Otto in *The Kingdom of God and the Son of Man.* The contribution of Dodd, therefore, was to set forth in its most persuasive form the contention that the Kingdom was actualized in Jesus' ministry and to endow this view with an aura of intellectual respectability.

The encomiums heaped over the years upon Professor Dodd's well-known book have been numerous. W. F. Howard, the Johannine scholar, in a 1937 article entitled "The Best Books on the Kingdom of God," referred to *The Parables of the Kingdom* as a "brilliant book."¹¹ Morna D. Hooker, Lady Margaret's Professor of Divinity in the University of Cambridge, in a lecture delivered in 1979 at Manchester University, remarked,

> The *Parables of the Kingdom* was an epoch-making book. It was an attempt to interpret the parables within the context of the ministry of Jesus. It is no exaggeration to describe the notion of realized eschatology upon

---

⁸Henry Burton Sharman, *The Teaching of Jesus about the Future* (Chicago, 1909) 306-309. Prolepses of the thesis presented in *The Parables of the Kingdom* can also be found in the following: Gerhard Kittel, "The This-Worldly Kingdom of God in Our Lord's Teaching," *Theology* 14 (May 1927): 261; E. F. Scott, "The Place of Apocalyptical Conceptions in the Mind of Jesus," *Journal of Biblical Literature* 41 (June 1922): 137-42; Harold Smith, "The Kingdom of God in the Ante-Nicene Fathers," *The Expository Times* 30 (March 1919): 248ff.

⁹William Manson, *Christ's View of the Kingdom of God* (London: James Clarke and Company, 1928) 57, 61, 81-84, 95, 158.

¹⁰Ibid., 97; italics added.

¹¹W. F. Howard, "The Best Books on the Kingdom of God," *The Expository Times* 48 (June 1937): 396.

which it is based as the most significant development this century in the discussion about the Kingdom of God.[12]

Moreover, in English universities and in American seminaries, beginning in the 1930s and 1940s, scores of New Testament scholars (and their students) became "realized eschatologists." Dodd's hypothesis became a hermeneutical fad; to be a devotee of realized eschatology was to be on the cutting edge of biblical research. The unreserved, enthusiastic acceptance realized eschatology has enjoyed is reflected in A. M. Hunter's evaluation as found in his *Introducing New Testament Theology,* a book written in popular style that (according to its author) contained "the latest theological insights and emphases." Referring to the "mystery" (Mark 4:11) of the Kingdom of God, Hunter wrote,

> Jesus believed the Kingdom of God to be present in himself and his Ministry—present in a "mystery" (Mark 4:11), indeed, but none the less really and dynamically present. . . . But the secret, the mystery—what is it? *In technical terms it is the meaning of "realized eschatology" and the meaning of the Messianic Ministry of Jesus are one and the same. In simple terms, the career of Jesus as the Servant Messiah, from Jordan to Calvary, is the Kingdom of God.* God acting in his royal power, God visiting and redeeming his People. For the Kingdom of God is no earthly empire to be set up by a political *coup d'etat.* It is the Kingdom in which God rules redeemingly through the Ministry of Jesus: not something added to the Ministry, but the Ministry itself. . . . *Jesus believed the Kingdom to be a present reality in himself and his Ministry. Indeed the evidence of the Gospels leaves us no option.*[13]

The preceding quotation should not be regarded as anomalous; rather, a study of literature dealing with synoptic eschatology will reveal scores of books and journal articles wherein there is agreement with Dodd's views concerning the Kingdom of God.[14] Dissenters, such as Morton Scott Ens-

---

[12]Morna D. Hooker, "New Testament Scholarship: Its Significance and Abiding Worth," *Bulletin of the John Rylands Library* 43 (Spring 1981): 426.

[13]Archibald M. Hunter, *Introducing New Testament Theology* (Philadelphia: Westminster Press, 1957) 23-27. Italics mine.

[14]A. W. Argyle, "The New Testament Interpretation of the Death of our Lord," *The Expository Times* 40 (June 1949): 253; "Does Realized Eschatology Make Sense?" *Hibbert Journal* 51 (July 1953): 387; C. K. Barrett, "New Testament Eschatology," *Scottish*

lin, who wrote that he neither "enthuses over" nor understands realized eschatology, have been few in number.[15]

Realized eschatology's appeal to Anglo-American exegetes is understandable. This hypothesis could be used to mitigate the view of "consistent eschatologists" such as Albert Schweitzer and Charles Guignebert, who contended that Jesus was mistaken in his expectations about the future. The unfeigned adoption of Dodd's hypothesis because it was deemed preferable to the views of Charles Guignebert is seen in the following quotation from an article by Paul Minear.

> The "realized eschatology" of C. H. Dodd is to be preferred to the thoroughgoing futurist apocalyptic of Charles Guignebert. For Dodd begins with the assurance that the Kingdom was a reality for Jesus; Guignebert treats it as only a pious and misguided wish. It is surely more accurate to hold that for Jesus the Kingdom belonged to the order of fact than to attribute it to the order of fancy. . . . The incongruity of apocalypticism to modern faith has made many Protestants receptive to the hypothesis of Mr. Dodd. It has seemed to preserve Jesus from the failures of prediction and the ravages of historical relativity.[16]

Journal of Theology 6 (September 1953): 230-31; C. J. Cadoux, *The Life of Jesus* (West Drayton: Penguin Books Ltd., 1948) 78; George S. Duncan, *Jesus, Son of Man* (London: James Nisbet and Company, 1948) 46-47; Floyd V. Filson, *One Lord One Faith* (Philadelphia: Westminster Press, 1943) 96-97; R. Newton Flew, "Jesus and the Kingdom of God," *The Expository Times* 46 (February 1935): 216; *Jesus and His Church* (London: Epworth Press, 1938), 20-24; S. Maclean Gilmour, *The Gospel Jesus Preached* (Philadelphia: Westminster Press, 1959) 86-91; Archibald M. Hunter, *The Work and Words of Jesus* (Philadelphia: Westminster Press, 1950) 68-74; Howard Clark Kee and Franklin W. Young, *Understanding the New Testament* (Englewood Cliffs: Prentice Hall, 1957) 118-27; Charles M. Laymon, *The Life and Teachings of Jesus* (New York: Abingdon Press, 1955) 170-72; Otto A. Piper, "The Mystery of the Kingdom of God," *Interpretation* 1 (April 1947): 187-200; Alan Richardson, "Kingdom of God," *A Theological Wordbook of the Bible* (New York: Macmillan, 1950) 119-21; *The Miracle-Stories of the Gospels* (London: SCM Press, 1941) 41; Harold Roberts, *Jesus and the Kingdom of God* (London: Epworth Press, 1955) 24-29; Vincent Taylor, *Jesus and His Sacrifice* (London: Macmillan, 1937) 6-11; William E. Wilson, "The Kingdom of God in This World," *Anglican Theological Review* 28 (October 1946): 181-82.

[15]Morton Scott Enslin, "Twixt the Dusk and the Daylight," *Journal of Biblical Literature* 75 (March 1956): 20.

[16]Paul S. Minear, "Time and the Kingdom," *The Journal of Religion* 24 (April 1944): 86, 87.

Thus realized eschatology serves an apologetic function.[17] Jesus is preserved "from the failures of prediction and the ravages of historical relativity." That realized eschatology was originally intended to be a contra-Schweitzer view is evident from an observation Professor Dodd made in his preface to the 1961 revised edition of *The Parables of the Kingdom.* "This book," he wrote,

> is based on a course of Shaffer Lectures given in the Divinity School, Yale University, in the spring of 1935. It was the product of an effort, sustained over several years, to come to terms with the problem of eschatology in the Gospels, particularly as it bears upon the idea of the Kingdom of God. At the time when I began serious study of the New Testament this problem had been forced into the centre of discussion, above all through the powerful influence of Albert Schweitzer. After his *Quest of the Historical Jesus* it was no longer possible to dispose of difficult eschatological passages by declaring them unauthentic or treating them as marginal and unimportant. The problem of eschatology is still with us, though the aspect under which it is now approached may be somewhat different. My work began by being orientated to the problem as Schweitzer had stated it. In common with many others, while deeply impressed by his treatment, I found myself unconvinced by his own formula of "consequente Eschatologie." The clue, it seemed, was still to seek.[18]

Realized eschatology—it should be emphasized—made its appearance on the stage of New Testament studies as an alternative or counter-proposal to consistent eschatology. The field of New Testament studies,

---

[17]Relevant to statements such as the just-quoted Minear remark is a terse assertion by H. H. Rowley. Writing in regard to what he deemed the erroneous eschatological expectation of Jesus he observed, "That it was a mistaken expectation does not seem to be a sufficient reason to deny it to our Lord." H. H. Rowley, *The Relevance of Apocalyptic* (New York: Harper and Brothers, 1946) 119. Relevant also is an observation by Cecil John Cadoux. Pleading for objectivity in biblical studies, he wrote on pages 9-10 of *The Historic Mission of Jesus* (London: Lutterworth Press, 1941) as follows: "In studying the eschatological teaching of Jesus, for instance, we must not be swayed (so far as we can help it) by a natural desire to discover that he was wholly immune from the intellectual limitations of his day and never foretold an event which did not occur. The greatness of the Christian movement and the authority of its Creeds must not be brought in to block plain and simple inferences from the gospel-evidence as it lies before us."

[18]This quotation appears on p. vii of the revised edition of *The Parables of the Kingdom* (New York: Charles Scribner's Sons, 1961).

however, is full of surprises. A surprising, unexpected development in biblical scholarship occurred when exegetes proposed: *Why not combine realized eschatology with consistent eschatology?* Instead of *either* realized eschatology *or* consistent eschatology, why not *both* realized eschatology *and* consistent eschatology? Students of early Christian origins reasoned as follows: "Schweitzer was right in what he said, but he went too far. Dodd was right in what he said, but he went too far also. We shall synthesize their views and recognize that for Jesus the Kingdom was *both* present *and* future." Scores of theologians adopted what C. K. Barrett called a "mediating position."[19] The mediating theologians heap praises upon Schweitzer, they heap praises upon Dodd, and they then declare that we now perceive (thanks to scholars like Schweitzer and Dodd) that for Jesus the Kingdom was *both a future hope and a present reality.* Thus, Vincent Taylor suggested that "discussions as to whether the kingdom is present or future are barren; it is obviously both."[20] It is in this attenuated form as found in writings by mediating theologians that Dodd's realized eschatology theory has exerted its greatest influence. Richard Hiers was right in observing that for the past decade or two "the dominant hypothesis" in New Testament studies "has been that the historical Jesus thought and proclaimed that the Kingdom of God was both future and, in some sense, present."[21]

This both-present-and-future view has become a routine ingredient in contemporary systematic theology. In 1979 Langdon Gilkey published a "baby" systematic theology that he entitled *Message and Existence: An Introduction to Christian Theology.* The following quotation from Professor Gilkey's book illustrates the way contemporary theologians view the Kingdom of God as both present and future.

> As is clear from all the "authentic" sayings of Jesus about the Kingdom, there are two distinguishable polarities central to this image, symbol, or concept. First of all, it had clearly a future reference: it was coming, about

---

[19]C. K. Barrett, "New Testament Eschatology," *Scottish Journal of Theology* 6 (June 1953): 155. Mr. Barrett pointedly observed that one of the characteristics of the "mediating position" is the error of vagueness.

[20]Taylor, *Jesus and His Sacrifice,* 9.

[21]Richard Hiers, *The Kingdom of God in the Synoptic Tradition* (Gainesville: University of Florida Press, 1970) 3.

to come, beginning to dawn—and it soon would be fully manifest (Luke 11:2, 22:18; Mark 14:25; Matt. 6:10; Luke 11:2; Matt. 8:11; Luke 3:28-29). On the other hand, in Jesus' deeds and words it was beginning already to be present, "in your midst," already under way (Mark 3:27; Luke 7:22, 10:18, 10:23, 11:20; Matt. 11:12, 12:28; Luke 17:20). A great deal of scholarly argument has taken place whether the Kingdom is simply future or whether it is "realized," already there, so to speak, with Jesus' appearance in history. At present, representatives of the two sides appear to agree that both emphases are present in the authentic words and parables of Jesus: the Kingdom is now beginning or about to come; its full manifestation lies in the near future, but with Jesus' life, action, and preaching, it is starting, "in your midst." As Reginald Fuller sums this up: "The message of Jesus proclaims the proleptic presence of the future Kingdom of God."[22]

One could cite many quotations from books and journal articles similar to the statement of Professor Gilkey just cited. That Jesus thought of the Kingdom as both present and future is (at least in Anglo-American theological circles) one of the "assured results" of life-of-Jesus research. This view has become a part of a Christian catechism currently in use in both Protestant and Roman Catholic churches.[23] At the 1988 General Conference in St. Louis this both-present-and-future view became the official position of the United Methodist Church. The *Book of Discipline* of the United Methodist Church contains a section entitled "Doctrinal Standards and Our Theological Task." Proposed for this section at the 1988 General Conference was the following assertion: "With other Christians we recognize that the Kingdom of God is both a present and future reality. The church is called to be that place where the first signs of the Kingdom are identified and acknowledged in the world." However, during the General Conference's deliberations in St. Louis the statement was modified to read: "With other Christians we recognize that the reign of God is both a present

---

[22]Langdon Gilkey, *Message and Existence: An Introduction to Christian Theology* (New York: Winston-Seabury, 1979) 166-67.

[23]*The Common Catechism* (New York: Seabury Press, 1975) 124: "A tension between present and future is one of the main features of Jesus' preaching about the Kingdom of God. Sometimes he describes it as something of the present, sometimes as something in the future." (The publisher describes *The Common Catechism* as "the first common catechism or statement of religious belief produced jointly by theologians of the Protestant and Roman Catholic churches since the Reformation of the sixteenth century.")

and future reality. The church is called to be that place where the first signs of the reign of God are identified and acknowledged in the world." This decision to change "Kingdom" to "reign" is significant; later in this study the point will be emphasized that C. H. Dodd is the primary source of the widely held view that "Kingdom" should be translated as "reign."

But did the historical Jesus think of the Kingdom as being *both* present *and* future? Is realized eschatology—in either a "pure" or "mediated" form—true? Does it make sense? Or is realized eschatology a hermeneutical tour de force? To grapple with these questions is the task of this book. A half century has passed since the publication of *The Parables of the Kingdom,* the book wherein realized eschatology was first persuasively advanced. During this intervening half century, New Testament research has not stood still. New insights have emerged. Entrenched positions have been undermined. This ebb and flow within New Testament studies necessitates a constant rethinking of exegetical-theological views, and in the discussion that follows I invite you to join me in rethinking realized eschatology. I want us to begin our rethinking by taking note of some recent vicissitudes of the Two-Document Hypothesis. To some readers this may seem a curious, doctrinaire place to begin a rethinking of realized eschatology. Yet it is not. Professor Dodd allowed the Two-Document Hypothesis to play a crucial role in his construction of realized eschatology. The Two-Document Hypothesis is a foundation stone undergirding *The Parables of the Kingdom.* Realized eschatology (that is, the Kingdom version thereof), I shall argue, is built upon a no-longer-certain theory of synoptic sources.

CHAPTER
• 2 •

A Critique of Dodd's Utilization of the Two-Document Hypothesis in *The Parables of the Kingdom*

I. The Pivotal Role of the Two-Document Hypothesis in *The Parables of the Kingdom*

The Synoptic Gospels contain approximately one hundred statements (including the parables) that Jesus made concerning the Kingdom of God. A scholar's understanding of what Jesus meant by the Kingdom will obviously be influenced by which of these statements he emphasizes. Also (and this is an insight that is frequently overlooked) a scholar's interpretation will be influenced by which of these approximately one hundred statements he ignores or deems to be secondary. In other words, literary criticism and theological interpretation are intertwined.[1] It is not out of order, therefore, for us to consider carefully *which* synoptic materials Professor Dodd *emphasized* while constructing his theory of realized eschatology. Likewise, we should note *which* synoptic materials *he ignored or passed over*. To do this we must turn our attention to the Two-Document (or Two-Source) Hypothesis, observing the crucial role it plays in *The Parables of the Kingdom*.

During the nineteenth century and into the opening decades of the present century, New Testament researchers were busily engaged in a quest

---

[1]C. C. McCown, *The Search for the Real Jesus* (New York: Charles Scribner's Sons, 1940) 213.

for literary sources believed to lie behind the Synoptic Gospels. This investigation was based on a theory of direct literary dependence. Scholars believed the Gospels were compilations of anterior literary sources, and they believed a patient, meticulous study of the Synoptics would result in the isolation of these sources. Scholars participated in this quest for earlier sources with the hope that their isolation would make possible a recovery of Jesus' thought unencumbered with and undistorted by the theology of the Christian community.[2] A cursory examination of such works as Sir John Hawkins's *Horae synopticae: Contributions to the Study of the Synoptic Problem* (1899, ²1909, ʳᵖᵗ1968), and B. H. Streeter's *The Four Gospels: A Study of Origins* (1924, ⁴1930, ¹⁰1961) will reveal the incredible amount of mental energy expended in behalf of the theory of direct literary dependence. The outcome of this quest was a practically unanimous agreement among scholars that Mark and "Q" (a supposed collection of "sayings" of Jesus) were anterior literary sources for Matthew and Luke.

A reading of *The Parables of the Kingdom* and of Dodd's journal articles reveals that during the 1920s and 1930s Dodd, like most other New Testament scholars at the time, was an enthusiastic supporter of the Two-Document Hypothesis. For example, in an article entitled "Present Tendencies in the Criticism of the Gospels" he wrote concerning documentary analysis:

> After long investigation and discussion, certain main conclusions emerged: that of the three Mark was the earliest, and was presupposed as

---

[2]Van A. Harvey, *The Historian and the Believer* (New York: Macmillan, 1969). To the point is a remark by Professor Harvey: referring to "a century long effort to establish the exact nature of New Testament sources," he wrote that "This effort was particularly important to the theologians of the Ritschlian school, who dominated Protestant theology in the last quarter of the century. It was essential to the Ritschlians that the Gospel tradition about Jesus be trustworthy, because the object of faith, they thought, is not the dogma of classical orthodoxy but the God-consciousness of Jesus, the force of his religious personality by which he had won a victory over the world. This, in part, accounts for the expenditure of so much energy on the Synoptic problem. Although it was not a victory easily achieved, the widespread consensus at the turn of the century was that Mark was the First Gospel, that it was, in either oral or written form, used by Matthew and Luke, and that the Fourth Gospel could not—or only with extreme caution—be used as a source for historical claims about Jesus. On the basis of this literary solution, it was believed, as Wilhelm Bousset wrote at the time, that there only remained to draw a 'life-like portrait which, with a few bold strokes, should bring out clearly the originality, the personality of Jesus' " (10-11).

a source by the other two, and that besides Mark a second written source, often denominated Q, was employed by Matthew and Luke. *This "two document hypothesis" has stood the test of time. It has maintained itself against attack from every conceivable quarter, and it does not seem likely that it will ever be successfully challenged.* Recent work on source criticism, such as that of Canon Streeter and Professor Bacon, while it may modify some accepted ideas of the sources, and certainly carries analysis further in profitable ways, *builds upon the two document hypothesis and leaves it more secure than ever.* Mark and Q remain our two fundamental sources for the life and teaching of Jesus.[3]

With regard to Q, Dodd wrote in 1925 "that such a document existed can scarcely be doubted by anyone competent to judge who takes the trouble to make a real examination of the data."[4] "Mark and Q remain the pillars of the historicity of the gospels."[5] The conclusion is obvious: Dodd unreservedly accepted the Two-Document Hypothesis.

The opinion of any scholar on critical problems is determined to a large extent by the temper of the time in which he lives. That Dodd accepted the Two-Document Hypothesis when he wrote *The Parables of the Kingdom* is not surprising. But what is not commonly recognized is Dodd's *extensive utilization of this hypothesis* in the working out of his theory of realized eschatology.

The critical judgment of the time that "Mark and the Book of Sayings are now generally recognized as the pillars of our knowledge of the life and teaching of Jesus"[6] permeates *The Parables of the Kingdom*. This book contains a plethora of references to Q.[7] Mark and Q are repeatedly referred to in a laudatory way as the "two best sources"[8] or as composing the ear-

---

[3] C. H. Dodd, "Present Tendencies in the Criticism of the Gospels," *The Expository Times* 43 (February 1932): 246.

[4] C. H. Dodd, "The Present Position of the Synoptic Problem," *Congregational Quarterly* 13 (April 1925): 209.

[5] Ibid., 211.

[6] C. H. Dodd, *The Bible and Its Background* (London: Unwin, ᵀᵖ1983, ¹1931) 773.

[7] C. H. Dodd, *The Parables of the Kingdom* (London: James Nisbet and Company, 1935) 32, 39, 40-42, 45, 48, 52, 60, 62, 64, 65, 69, 72, 81, 83-87, 89, 90, 93-95, 143, 144, 158, 167, 169, 170, 179, 189, 191.

[8] Ibid., 53, 59.

lier or earliest sources and traditions for a study of Jesus' thought.[9] When a given item occurs in both Mark and Q, the reader is informed that this is "the strongest form of attestation which our Gospels can provide."[10] Dodd's most extensive discussion of synoptic sources in *The Parables of the Kingdom* is found at the beginning of the book's second chapter. Consensual with earlier published evaluations Dodd asserted that

> We are therefore left with Mark and Q as primary sources, and I do not think criticism has yet provided us with any better *organon* for approximating to the original tradition of the words and works of Jesus than is supplied by a careful study and comparison of these two.[11]

This discussion of synoptic sources closes with an observation by Professor Dodd that demands scrutiny:

> In dealing therefore with the complicated question of the Kingdom of God, we shall not only be saving time by leaving out of account (with few exceptions) those parts of Matthew and Luke which have no parallel in other Gospels, but we shall be dealing with material which has the best claim to bring us in touch with the earliest tradition accessible to us at all.[12]

In this methodological statement by Dodd it is important to note that in the interest of "saving time" and because he considered the subject of the Kingdom of God to be complex, Dodd proposed a *limitation of synoptic evidence to Mark and Q*.[13] Thus, the theory of realized eschatology was constructed by Dodd upon data *drawn exclusively from Mark and Q*. This Mark-Q criterion became in Dodd's hands a critical device for selecting

---

[9]Ibid., 33, 49, 56, 58, 83, 84, 85, 88, 89, 91, 96, 104, 115.

[10]Ibid., 33; 20 in 1961 rev. ed.

[11]Ibid., 40 (26 in 1961 rev. ed.).

[12]Ibid., 41 (27 in 1961 rev. ed.).

[13]It is to be noted from the quotation just cited that the Mark-Q circumscription was to be followed "with few exceptions." It is difficult to resist the suspicion, however, that Dodd gave attention to passages that were not in Mark or Q *only* when it was in the interest of his theory to do so. The best example of this prejudicious use of evidence is Dodd's discussion (ibid., 84-85) of Luke 17:20-21, a passage that easily lends itself to an abstract understanding of the Kingdom that Dodd favored.

materials. Synoptic evidence *outside* these two sources was ignored.[14] This fact cannot be emphasized too strongly. Throughout *The Parables of the Kingdom* synoptic material was deemed relevant or irrelevant, reliable or unreliable, *by whether or not it appeared in Mark or Q*. Professor Dodd, employing a Mark-Q circumscription of evidence, excluded from his discussion a vast amount of synoptic data concerning the Kingdom.[15]

This Mark-Q circumscription, however, made it possible for Professor Dodd to ignore provocative material in the Synoptics concerning the Kingdom. For example, the five passages below, selected at random, are not dealt with at all in *The Parables of The Kingdom*.

---

[14]Dodd's dependence in *The Parables of the Kingdom* on the Two-Document Hypothesis was recognized but not elaborated by Dom Christopher Butler in "Three Books on the New Testament," *Downside Review* 65 (October 1947): 344. In this article Butler wittily expressed his longing for the time when the Two-Document Hypothesis would be nothing more than "a museum specimen" of the "neolithic age of criticism."

[15]In this regard I call to your attention the following *partial* listing of (1) passages that Dodd excluded from discussion in *The Parables of the Kingdom* and (2) passages that he deemed to be of only secondary importance. (In the second list the numbers in parentheses indicate the pages of *The Parables of the Kingdom* where Dodd disparages these "secondary" passages.)

(1) Passages excluded from discussion: Matthew 5:19-20; 6:10 (∥ Luke 11:2); 7:21; 13:43, 52; 16:28 (∥ Luke 9:27); 18:4; 19:12; 20:20-23 (the parallel at Mark 10:35-40 is cited by Dodd not with reference to the Kingdom but to illustrate that Jesus predicted persecution for his followers); 21:43; Mark 9:47; 10:23-24 (∥ Matthew 19:23-24 ∥ Luke 18:24-25); 11:10; 15:43 (∥ Luke 23:50-52); Luke 9:1-2; 12:32-34; 14:15; 19:11; 21:29-33.

(2) Passages treated as secondary: Matthew 3:2 (48); 13:36-43 (183); 13:49-50 (187); 18:23-35 (33); 25:34 (85); Luke 22:17-18 (56); 22:28-30 (72-74). (Note that while important passages in Mark are excluded from discussion, no Markan passages appear in the "secondary" listing.)

Dodd disparaged the Matthean account of the ministry of John the Baptist (Matthew 3:2), but it will be shown in the next chapter that this verse presents one of the crucial arguments against Dodd's equation of ἐγγίζω with φθάνω.

It also will be necessary in the discussion that follows to reexamine briefly data that Dodd interpreted in terms of Platonic philosophy. E.g., in his discussion of Matthew 8:11 he suggested that in this verse "the patriarchs are thought of as living 'in the Kingdom of God,' in the world beyond this, where God's Kingdom does not 'come,' but is eternally present" (*The Parables of the Kingdom,* 55). With reference to the logion of Mark 14:25 ("I will never again drink of the fruit of the vine until that day when I drink it new in the Kingdom of God") Dodd asked, "Are we to think of the Kingdom of God here as something yet to come? If so, it is not to come in this world, for the 'new wine' belongs to the 'new heaven and new earth' of apocalyptic thought, that is, to the transcendent order beyond space and time" (ibid., 56).

> Whosoever then relaxes one of the least of these commandments and teaches men so, shall be called least in the kingdom of heaven; but he who does them and teaches them shall be called great in the kingdom of heaven. For I tell you, unless your righteousness exceeds that of the scribes and Pharisees, you will never enter the kingdom of heaven.
> (Matthew 5:19-20)
>
> Not every one who says to me, "Lord, Lord," shall enter the kingdom of heaven, but he who does the will of my Father who is in heaven.
> (Matthew 7:21)
>
> Whoever humbles himself like this child, he is the greatest in the kingdom of heaven. (Matthew 18:4)
>
> So also, when you see these things taking place, you know that the kingdom of God is near. (Luke 21:31)
>
> And he said to them, "I have earnestly desired to eat this passover with you before I suffer; for I tell you I shall not eat it until it is fulfilled in the kingdom of God." (Luke 22:15-16)[16]

In *The Parables of the Kingdom,* as the next chapter will show, Dodd argued that the Kingdom (*basileia*) was an abstract power operative in Jesus' exorcisms. The five statements quoted above do not lend themselves to this dynamic understanding of *basileia.* Yet for Dodd the exclusion (or ignoring) of these five statements from his discussion was methodologically justifiable because they do not appear in his two prime sources—Mark and Q.

If this critical-literary device (the Two-Document Hypothesis) used pervasively by Dodd was not a valid one, however, then clearly a methodological error lies at the heart of *The Parables of the Kingdom.* That is the argument I am making in this chapter. Since the publication of *The Parables of the Kingdom* in 1935, the world of New Testament scholarship has witnessed the dethroning (if not disproving) of the Two-Document Hypothesis. The line of reasoning presented by Professor Dodd in *The Parables of the Kingdom,* I want to suggest, is constructed upon a questionable critical judgment; at the book's core is a structural fault—an exaggerated, exclusive dependence upon Mark and Q with a concomitant ignoring of evidence outside Mark and Q.

---

[16]In *The Parables of the Kingdom* Luke 22:15-16 was relegated to a footnote (p. 56; 39 in 1961 rev. ed.) and was described as being "secondary."

II. The Dethroning of the Two-Document Hypothesis

Time and again scholars have given the impression that the synoptic problem is a closed issue—closed because it was solved once and for all by earlier source critics such as Professor B. H. Streeter. Indeed, throughout most of the present century, seminary professors and college teachers have taught the Two-Document Hypothesis to their students as though this hypothesis was handed down at Mount Sinai—immutable, unquestionable, engraved on tablets of stone. "From now until the end of time *the solution* of the synoptic problem is: Mark is the earliest gospel and was used by Matthew and Luke. Matthew and Luke also used Q, a sayings source."

Amazingly enough, however, the world of biblical studies is experiencing today a reawakening of synoptic source criticism.[17] This reawakening is a well-kept secret in New Testament circles. Professors in scores of institutions continue to teach the Two-Document Hypothesis as though a man named Hans-Herbert Stoldt never lived, and participants at annual meetings of the American Academy of Religion continue to deliver papers bearing such titles as "The Christology of Q" and "Was Q a Syrian Document?" They read these papers unaware that their reasoning may be based on quicksand.

An event serving as well as any other to signal this reopening of the synoptic question was the 1964 publication of Professor W. R. Farmer's *The Synoptic Problem: A Critical Analysis,* a work that sought "to demonstrate that the idea of Marcan priority is highly questionable."[18] For

---

[17]M.-E. Boismard, "The Two-Source Theory at an Impasse," *New Testament Studies* 26 (October 1979): 1-17. Boismard began this article by stating, "Twenty years ago we could assume that the Two-Source theory, as the decisive solution to the synoptic problem, had won the day. An unassailable dogma in Germany, on the front lines in Louvain, well positioned in England and the United States, it had little to fear from the last spasms of its opponents, and could view them as the final stand of the rearguard. But times have changed. Aged Griesbach turns in his grave, refusing to stay defeated. After two centuries he has returned to the field in the persons of Dom Butler of England and, especially, of W. R. Farmer of the United States, who has succeeded in mustering a force of young and dynamic researchers. Even in Germany the enemy has gained a foothold. Already in 1971 A. Fuchs saw that a large number of the Matthew/Luke agreements against Mark could not be explained in terms of the Two-Source theory. More recently, H. H. Stoldt has affirmed his preference for the Griesbach theory." (References omitted.)

[18]William R. Farmer, *The Synoptic Problem* (New York: Macmillan, 1964; corrected rpt.: Dillsboro NC: Western North Carolina Press, 1976) vii. (This book is now available from Mercer University Press, Macon GA.)

Professor Farmer (of Perkins School of Theology, Southern Methodist University) to question Markan priority as he did was courageous. The Markan hypothesis (Mark is the earliest gospel and was a literary source for Matthew and Luke) had been a cornerstone of synoptic criticism since the days of Heinrich Julius Holtzmann, whose study on the Synoptics appeared in 1863.

To explore *in detail* reasons recently leveled against the Markan hypothesis by scholars like Professor Farmer is beyond the purview of this book. The published material on this issue has become voluminous, and the arguments at times are difficult to follow. At this point in our discussion I am presupposing research and argumentation presented in Pierson Parker's *The Gospel Before Mark*[19] and B. C. Butler's *The Originality of St. Matthew: A Critique of the Two-Document Hypothesis*.[20] I am presupposing argumentation found in *The Relationships among the Gospels: An Interdisciplinary Dialogue*,[21] *New Synoptic Studies: The Cambridge Gospel Conference and Beyond*,[22] and *Colloquy on New Testament Studies: A Time for Reappraisal and Fresh Approaches*.[23] I am presupposing *The Two-Source Hypothesis: A Critical Appraisal* edited by Arthur J. Bellinzoni, Jr. (this important anthology contains twenty-eight essays, some supportive of the Two-Document Hypothesis, some critical of the Two-Document Hypothesis).[24] Above all I am presupposing Hans-Herbert Stoldt's *History*

---

[19]Pierson Parker, *The Gospel Before Mark* (Chicago: University of Chicago Press, 1953).

[20]B. C. Butler, *The Originality of St. Matthew: A Critique of the Two-Document Hypothesis* (London: Cambridge University Press, 1951). That B. C. Butler's book should be taken seriously is reflected in Austin Farrer's review that appeared in *The Journal of Theological Studies* 3 (April 1952) 102-106. On page 106 he wrote, "Here is a writer who demolishes the Q hypothesis, and submits the current views about Marcan priority to the most searching criticism they have yet undergone. If he does not overthrow Marcan priority, he puts it on its mettle, and forces its defenders to make a serious reconsideration of the way in which the two oldest gospels were conceived and composed by their inspired authors."

[21]William O. Walker, Jr., ed., *The Relationships among the Gospels: An Interdisciplinary Dialogue* (San Antonio: Trinity University Press, 1978).

[22]William R. Farmer, ed., *New Synoptic Studies: The Cambridge Gospel Conference and Beyond* (Macon GA: Mercer University Press, 1983).

[23]Bruce Corley, ed., *Colloquy on New Testament Studies: A Time for Reappraisal and Fresh Approaches* (Macon GA: Mercer University Press, 1983).

[24]Arthur J. Bellinzoni, ed., *The Two-Source Hypothesis: A Critical Appraisal* (Macon GA: Mercer University Press, 1985).

and Criticism of the Marcan Hypothesis[25] and two books by Professor W. R. Farmer—*The Synoptic Problem*[26] and *Jesus and the Gospel.*[27] Any person who wants to understand what is going on today in synoptic source criticism must mentally digest the evidence and argumentation found in these books. Moreover, any person who reflectively works through this evidence and argumentation will find it impossible to refer glibly to the Markan hypothesis as still an "assured result" of nineteenth-century synoptic criticism. Such is the case because objections raised by these cited works against Marcan priority are both legion and potent.

By way of example, the Marcan hypothesis is contrary to external evidence (for patristic data are unanimous in placing Matthew chronologically prior to Mark).[28] The Marcan hypothesis does not harmonize with first-century Christianity's historical development (an insight worked out in detail by Professor Farmer in *Jesus and the Gospel*).[29] Beginning as a Jewish sect, the Church underwent a "gentilization" process during the course of which a predominantly Jewish movement became a predominantly non-Jewish movement. Thus an obvious inadequacy of the Marcan hypothesis "is that it offers no explanation for its requirement that the more Jewish and Palestinian Gospel, Matthew, must be perceived as coming after

---

[25]Hans-Herbert Stoldt, *History and Criticism of the Marcan Hypothesis*, trans. and ed. Donald Niewyk, intro. by William R. Farmer (Macon GA: Mercer University Press, 1980). This work was originally published in German with the title *Geschichte und Kritik der Markushypothese* (Göttingen: Vandenhoeck & Ruprecht, 1977).

[26]See n. 1 above.

[27]William R. Farmer, *Jesus and the Gospel: Tradition, Scripture, and Canon* (Philadelphia: Fortress Press, 1982).

[28]In ibid. Farmer develops this insight *in extenso,* particularly on pp. 93-110. He observes, "Moreover, all the church fathers who mention the sequence in which the Gospels were written indicate that Matthew came first. The earliest statement regarding sequence was made by Clement of Alexandria who indicated that both Matthew and Luke were written before Mark. A commonplace of sound historiography is for the historian to balance internal with external evidence. An inadequacy of the theory of Marcan priority is that it does not maintain such a balance. Those who defend Marcan priority ignore their responsibility to account for the fact that there is little or no support for it from external evidence." Professor Farmer's point is well-taken. Patristic writers like Clement of Alexandria, Origen, and Augustine are of one mind in placing Matthew prior to Mark. No patristic writer clearly supports a theory of Marcan priority.

[29]Ibid., 6-11.

and as dependent upon the less Jewish and less Palestinian Mark. This is a historical difficulty of very great consequence."³⁰

Moreover, during the past century the argument has been repeatedly advanced that Mark's primitivity was "proven" by the argument from order.³¹ Yet Professor Farmer has resurrected B. C. Butler's "Lachmann fallacy" and has convincingly demonstrated in *The Synoptic Problem* that the argument from order is a logical non sequitur.³² He has also reopened the debate concerning the minor agreements of Matthew and Luke against Mark, a phenomenon once referred to by Morton Scott Enslin as "probably the crux of the whole problem of the relationship of our gospels."³³ Furthermore, scholars like Pierson Parker have plausibly argued that Mark's *secondary nature* is demonstrated by its scriptural misquotations, its geographical puzzles, its historical mistakes, its pro-Gentile sympathies (which led Rudolf Bultmann to describe Mark as the "gospel for Gentile Christianity"), its apologetic inserts (such as *das Messiasgeheimnis*—the "messianic secret"—motif), and its miracle-story embellishments (which suggest—as Schleiermacher contended—affinities between Mark and the

---

³⁰Ibid., 9.

³¹Weaknesses inherent in this argument are discussed by Malcolm Lowe, "The Demise of Arguments from Order for Markan Priority," *Novum Testamentum* 24 (January 1982): 27-36.

³²Farmer, *The Synoptic Problem*, 63-66. Farmer suggests, "But if Matthew, Mark, and Luke are directly related to one another rather than being indirectly related through some earlier source which all three have independently copied, then the phenomenon of order no more supports the priority of Mark than priority of Matthew or Luke" (66). Professor Farmer devotes several pages to the profound yet unfortunate influence of a paper read at Oxford in 1886 by F. H. Woods. The paper was entitled "The Origin and Mutual Relation of the Synoptic Gospels." With reference to Woods's paper Professor Farmer observed, "The effect of Woods's essay, therefore, was to narrow the gap between Ur-Marcus and Mark to practical insignificance—and to pave the way for Streeter's logical fallacy of thinking that the argument from order still held after the idea of an Ur-Marcus had been completely abandoned and Matthew and Luke were conceived to be directly dependent on the text of Mark. Here is a germinal seed of one of the most calamitous misconceptions in the history of the Synoptic Problem" (65). Further regarding Woods's paper Professor Farmer pointed out that "Here is the earliest evidence of an error that B. C. Butler sixty-five years later was to term the Lachmann fallacy" (66).

³³Morton Scott Enslin, *Christian Beginnings* (New York: Harper & Brothers, 1938) 430.

apocryphal gospels).[34] Particularly devastating to the Marcan hypothesis is the reductio ad absurdum argument presented in the first chapter of Hans-Herbert Stoldt's *History and Criticism of the Marcan Hypothesis*. In this discussion Stoldt presents in agonizing, meticulous detail the problems inherent in the view that Mark is prior to and was a source for Matthew and Luke.[35]

I am not suggesting the Marcan priority hypothesis has been disproved. This theory, given the incompleteness of the data, cannot be disproven. Yet hypotheses, although maybe not falsifiable, can suffer depletions of plausibility. The Marcan hypothesis has suffered a plausibility depletion. The arguments of the Stoldts and Farmers *against* Marcan priority are as convincing as arguments of the Holtzmanns and Streeters *for* Marcan priority. Thus the primitivity of the second gospel has become again an open question, not a closed one, and Marcan priority can no longer be used by exegetes as an "unquestionable" hermeneutical tool. That an abandonment of the Marcan priority theory triggers a collapse of the Two-Document Hypothesis goes without saying.

Likewise, in recent years scholars have reappraised the Q hypothesis. This theory, like Belshazzar, has been weighed in the balances and found wanting. In the interest of brevity I will not consider some arguments against the Q hypothesis: the minor agreements of Matthew and Luke against Mark that make the Q hypothesis unnecessary;[36] the absence of a unifying motif

---

[34]A concise presentation of Pierson Parker's view regarding Mark's lateness is found in his article "A Second Look at the Gospel Before Mark," *Journal of Biblical Literature* 100 (1981): 389-413.

[35]Hans-Herbert Stoldt discusses in the first chapter of his book (cited above in n. 25) problems inherent in the Marcan hypothesis. For example, he lists numerous instances where Matthew and Luke agree in wording contrary to Mark, and he cites numerous instances (some 180) where additional details in Mark extend beyond the texts of Matthew and Luke. In other words, Stoldt cites hundreds of synoptic details that are difficult to explain on the assumption that Mark is the earliest Gospel. These synoptic details he referred to as "liabilities" when he wrote, "It is apparent that the originators of the Marcan hypothesis took on a heavy burden when they tried to prove its validity without first considering these liabilities." Stoldt, *History and Criticism of the Marcan Hypothesis*, 22.

[36]D. M. Goulder, "On Putting Q to the Test," *New Testament Studies* 24 (January 1978): 218-34.

that makes every reconstruction of Q problematical;[37] the absence of a characteristic style of language;[38] or the clever reductio ad absurdum with regard to the conflation hypothesis advanced by B. C. Butler in *The Originality of St. Matthew*.[39] Instead, attention will be given to the *problem of order* and to the *problem of lack of word agreement* in passages traditionally assigned to Q. These represent the two crucial arguments against the Q hypothesis.

A study of relevant data reveals that many sections usually assigned to Q do *not* appear in Matthew and Luke *in the same order*. One of the most comprehensive discussions of this issue is found in E. W. Lummis's *How Luke Was Written*.[40] Writers on the synoptic problem fail to point out that lack of agreement in the order of Q material in Matthew and in Luke points *against* the Q hypothesis. Critics (like Streeter) *assumed* the unity of Q. Likewise, in *The Parables of the Kingdom* the unity of Q was presupposed. Dodd suggested repeatedly that Q was a literary source used by both Matthew and Luke, and because it is an anterior source it must be highly valued in any reconstruction of Jesus' thought. Yet, if approximately half the pericopes usually assigned to Q appear in different order in Matthew and Luke, this difference-in-order phenomenon does not suggest they were derived from a common source but from a number of disconnected sources or from oral tradition.

I have found this criticism of the Q hypothesis based on lack of agreement in order discussed by such scholars as Taylor, Barrett, Knox, and

---

[37]W. L. Knox, *The Sources of the Synoptic Gospels* (Cambridge: Cambridge University Press, 1957) 3-5. Pierson Parker (on p. 392 of his article cited in n. 34 above) observed, "Q is so deucedly amorphous and so lacking in any apparent purpose." With reference to Q reconstructions A. M. Farrer made the sardonic observation that "the postulation of unevidenced writing of an indeterminate sort is a hazardous proceeding." See p. 61 of A. M. Farrer, "On Dispensing with Q," in D. E. Nineham, ed., *Studies in the Gospels* (Oxford: Basil Blackwell, 1957). On p. 16 of *The Originality of St. Matthew* (cited in n. 20 above) B. C. Butler protested the "motiveless and extremely difficult patchwork composition" (a composition that is "psychologically and artistically" improbable) of Q as advocated by scholars such as B. H. Streeter.

[38]John C. Hawkins, *Horae Synopticae* (Oxford: Clarendon Press, 1909) 113.

[39]Butler, *The Originality of St. Matthew*, 1-22; "St. Luke's Debt to St. Matthew," *Harvard Theological Review* 32 (October 1939): 237-308.

[40]E. W. Lummis, *How Luke Was Written* (Cambridge: Cambridge University Press, 1915).

A Critique of Dodd • 25

Chapman,[41] but by far the most effective presentation of this argument that I have encountered was found in an unpublished doctoral dissertation by Marion Hostetler.[42] Mr. Hostetler, arguing that critics are not justified in glibly assuming the unity of Q, tabulated three parallel Q passages as follows:[43]

SYMBOL	REFERENCE	SUBJECT	REFERENCE	SYMBOL
D^M	MT 8:19-22	Discipleship	LK 9:57-60	D^L
G^M	MT 8:11-12	Gentiles in the Kingdom	LK 13:28-29	G^L
B^M	MT 13:16-17	Blessedness of Disciples	LK 10:23-24	B^L

From the similarity of D^M and D^L it is logical to deduce some relationship. There are three possibilities.

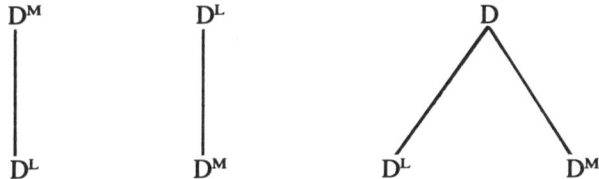

The third solution is the one adopted by Streeterian source critics. Both D^M and D^L were derived from D, a common source. Likewise, they deduce that G^M and G^L had a common source G, and that B^M and B^L came from a common source B. But an additional deduction is not warranted. *Because B, D, and G are common sources of Matthean and Lucan material, that*

---

[41]Vincent Taylor, "The Order of Q," *The Journal of Theological Studies* 4 (April 1953): 27-35; C. K. Barrett, "Q: A Re-Examination," *Expository Times* 54 (September 1943): 32-33; Knox, *The Sources of the Synoptic Gospels,* 4; Dom John Chapman, *Matthew, Mark, and Luke: A Study in the Order and Interrelation of the Synoptic Gospels* (London: Longmans, Green and Company, 1937) 96.

[42]Marion Stewart Hostetler, "The Place of B. H. Streeter in the Study of the Synoptic Problem" (Ph.D. diss., The Hartford Seminary Foundation, 1952).

[43]Ibid., 54.

does not prove that B, D, and G are themselves parts of one common source (Q). The parallelism just noted does possibly indicate this relationship:

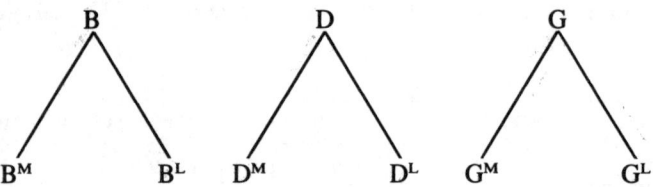

But the parallelism in the three noted passages does *not* demonstrate this relationship:

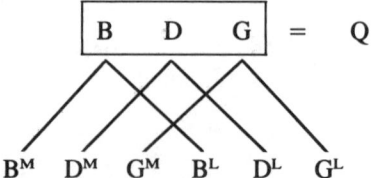

The unity of Q might possibly have been assumed if the pericopes assigned to Q had occurred in the same order in Matthew and Luke. But this is not the case. *The unity of the fragments that modern scholarship calls Q is an unproven hypothesis.* Thus to the point is the observation by Foakes-Jackson and Kirsopp Lake:

> It must be remembered that Q is not an extant document, but represents the judgment of critics as to certain parts of Matthew and Luke. It is impossible to reconstruct it mechanically, and it is a mistake to attribute a so-called objective value to what is after all the result of subjective criticism.[44]

In future investigations of the synoptic problem there can be no reversion to the position of earlier source critics who unjustifiably *assumed* the Q materials came from a *single document* analogous to Mark. Instead,

---

[44]F. J. Foakes-Jackson and Kirsopp Lake, *Prolegomena*, vol. 1 of *The Beginnings of Christianity*, 5 vols. (London: Macmillan, 1920), 268.

"future students of this material must begin from the *formgeschichtliche* dictum that the basic unit is the pericope."[45]

I want us now to give attention to a second pivotal argument against Q: the lack of word agreement in passages assigned to Q. There are passages traditionally ascribed to Q that have such widely differing Greek texts that to argue they originally came from the *same* document is a questionable critical judgment. I shall never forget the perplexity I experienced when I studied for the first time in a Huck's *Synopsis of the First Three Gospels* the passages traditionally assigned to Q. Between most of these parallel passages I could not perceive enough word-syntax similarity to justify the critical judgment that they were derived from a common literary source.

Because scholars cannot agree on the extent of linguistic agreement necessary to justify the ascription of parallel passages to Q, their reconstructions of Q vary considerably. James Moffatt in his classic *An Introduction to the Literature of the New Testament* gave no less than sixteen conjectured reconstructions of Q, and his list was by no means complete.[46] The failure of critics to agree on the content of Q fully justifies Vincent Taylor's jocular description of it as an "elusive" document.[47]

C. K. Barrett in an article entitled "Q: A Re-examination" leveled a pointed criticism against this willingness of source critics to designate as Q material parallel passages that have small degrees of syntactical-linguistic agreement. He observed that when Matthew and Luke are following Mark their agreement is greatest when they repeat the words of Jesus. It follows, therefore, that "since a great part of Q consists of sayings we should expect that the Matthean and Lukan forms of these sayings, if they were derived from a common source, would reveal the same verbal similarity."[48] Yet numerous sections traditionally assigned to the hypothetical Q source display a wide divergence of syntax and wording. Barrett illustrated this divergence with the Cheek-striking and Coat-seizure pericope (Matthew 5:39-40 || Luke 6:29).

---

[45]Hostetler, "Study of the Synoptic Problem," 84.

[46]James Moffat, *An Introduction to the Literature of the New Testament* (Edinburgh: T. & T. Clark, 1918) 197-202.

[47]Vincent Taylor, "The Elusive Q," *Expository Times* 46 (November 1934): 68-74.

[48]Barrett, "Q: A Re-examination," 321.

MATTHEW 5:39-40	LUKE 6:29
ἀλλ' ὅστις σε ῥαπίζει εἰς τὴν δεξιὰν σιαγόνα [σου], στρέψον αὐτῷ καὶ τὴν ἄλλην καὶ τῷ θέλοντί σοι κριθῆναι καὶ τὸν χιτῶνά σου λαβεῖν, ἄφες αὐτῷ καὶ τὸ ἱμάτιον.	τῷ τύπτοντί σε ἐπὶ τὴν σιαγόνα πάρεχε καὶ τὴν ἄλλην καὶ ἀπὸ τοῦ αἴροντός σου τὸ ἱμάτιον καὶ τὸν χιτῶνα μὴ κωλύσῃς.

The differences are many: ῥαπίζω versus τύπτω; the insertion of δεξιάν; στρέφω versus παρέχω; θέλω versus αἴρω; and ἄφες versus κωλύσῃς. Moreover, the coat seizure in Luke is presented as robbery, whereas in Matthew it is presented in the context of a lawsuit. The differences are too great to argue (as Q partisans do) that the *same written logion* has been subjected to both Matthean and Lukan editorial modification. Though substantially the same tradition, these two sections have evidently been transmitted independently of one another.

That *some* of the common matter in Matthew and Luke was derived by the authors of these two Gospels from the same source or sources is possible. T. W. Manson in *The Mission and Message of Jesus* has shown there is a measure of agreement in the Q reconstructions of Harnack, Streeter, and Bussman. During the course of my research for this book I studied the matter common to all three of these just-mentioned reconstructions. The sections that impress me as being so similar as to suggest direct literary relationship are Luke 3:7b-9; 7:8; 22:25a; 26-27; 9:57b-58; 10:2, 13-15, 21-22; 11:9-10, 31-32; 12:40; 13:34-35; 16:13 and their Matthean parallels—a total of some twenty-six verses. It does not at all follow, however, that these verses came from *one* common literary source.

The cumulative force of these arguments, I believe, is decisive against the Q hypothesis. Why try to understand parallel sections in Matthew and Luke as modifications of a common written source, when their *similarities* can more logically be understood as being due to parallel oral or written versions of the same event or saying, and their *dissimilarities* can more logically be understood as due to the authorial activity of the synoptic writers?

Indeed, a recognition of the authorial activity of the synoptic writers is a reminder that *the underlying methodological fallacy of scholars who postulated the Two-Document Hypothesis was their conception of the synoptic writers as anthologists*. The Streeterian source critics looked upon the authors of the Synoptic Gospels as adapters and compilers of literary sources.[49] To the source critics the Gospels were, to use the apt description of Hollis Huston, "scrapbooks of press clippings about Jesus."[50]

This approach to the synoptic problem found classic expression in Professor B. H. Streeter's complex conflation hypothesis which was elaborated in *The Four Gospels*. Since the creative days of source criticism, however, a change has taken place in our understanding of the nature of the Gospels. This change, destroying the premise from which the source critics approached the problem of synoptic relationships, has been due to *form criticism* and to a *recognition of the theological nature of the Gospels*.

Form criticism has made possible the insight that our Gospels are not exclusively compilations of literary sources but are also (in part) repositories of the preaching of the early Church.[51] Instead of ascribing all the gospel materials to different *literary sources* as the Streeterians did, form critics argue that at the time the Synoptics were written there were extant in various Christian circles floating oral traditions that the Synoptists employed in composing their Gospels. In a striking metaphor, Morton Scott Enslin referred to these available oral traditions as mines when he wrote,

> It would appear to me not unlikely that not only was it from these mines that Mark drew much of his ore, but that they were still being worked when Matthew and Luke girded themselves for their task.[52]

When he wrote *The Parables of the Kingdom,* Dodd was not unaware of form criticism that at that time was a new approach to synoptic data. References to this new methodology are found in *The Parables of the*

---

[49]A. M. Farrer, "On Dispensing with Q," in D. E. Nineham, ed., *Studies in the Gospels* (Oxford: Basil Blackwell, 1957) 56.

[50]Hollis Huston, "The 'Q Parties' at Oxford," *The Journal of Bible and Religion* 25 (April 1957): 127.

[51]Form criticism per se is not discussed in this chapter. There is a presupposing of the content of such books as Rudolf Bultmann, *History of the Synoptic Tradition,* trans. John Marsh (New York: Harper & Row, 1963); Edgar V. McKnight, *What is Form Criticism?* (Philadelphia: Fortress Press, 1969); Frederick C. Grant, *Form Criticism—A New Method of New Testament Research* (Chicago: University of Chicago Press, 1934); E. Basil Redlich, *Form Criticism—Its Value and Limitations* (London: Duckworth, 1939).

[52]Morton Scott Enslin, *Christian Beginnings* (New York: Harper & Row, 1956) 436.

Kingdom,[53] but Dodd did not anticipate (as Lightfoot did) the wide acceptance form criticism was to receive.[54] His personal evaluation of *Formgeschichte* during this period of his academic career can be seen in the following statement that appeared in an *Expository Times* article wherein Schmidt's *Der Rahmen der Geschichte Jesu,* Dibelius's *Formgeschichte des Evangeliums,* and Bultmann's *Geschichte der Synoptischen Tradition* were briefly discussed by Dodd:

> The school of *Formgeschichte* has not, I think it must be admitted, as yet produced a work of really first-class quality (unless we except K. L. Schmidt's book, which is rather preparatory to *Formgeschichte*), nor have its achieved results so far been commensurate with the *eclat* with which it has been announced. Its conclusions so far are very vulnerable.[55]

Dodd expressed a similar attitude in *The Parables of the Kingdom*.[56] This negative attitude on Dodd's part was a reflection of the hostile attitude existing at that time in English theological circles toward form criticism. The year of publication of *The Parables of the Kingdom* also witnessed the publication of R. H. Lightfoot's Bampton Lectures. In the preface to *History and Interpretation in the Gospels,* Lightfoot wrote with regard to form

---

[53]Dodd, *The Parables of the Kingdom,* 18, 23, 40, 104, 111, 116.

[54]In fairness to Dodd, however, it should be noted that after 1935 he changed his opinion toward synoptic literary analysis and form criticism. This can be seen clearly in his *According to the Scriptures* (New York: Charles Scribner's Sons, 1953) 29. Writing in a context wherein he argued that earlier criticism was wrong in supposing that the early Christians were a "bookish community," Dodd observed, "The main current of its life and thought seems to have been carried by oral tradition, at least to the end of the first century, and the surviving documents are, in large measure, the deposit of a common tradition in its various stages developed in one way or another according to the idiosyncrasy of the several authors. In certain specific cases indeed there is definite evidence that writings had some kind of literary connection, over and above the common tradition underlying them all, but except where some such evidence can be adduced, the presumption of literary dependence is precarious, since resemblances might be so probably accounted for without it."

[55]C. H. Dodd, "Present Tendencies in the Criticism of the Gospels," *Expository Times* 43 (February 1932): 248.

[56]Dodd, *The Parables of the Kingdom,* 40-41.

criticism, "I regret the suspicion and indeed hostility with which this study is regarded at present in this country, and I think it is mistaken."[57]

Thus when *The Parables of the Kingdom* was published, form criticism was a new methodology. Since then many of the skeptical value judgments of the form critics have been rejected. But the theory that the Gospels (at least in part) are repositories of oral traditions rather than mosaics of anterior literary sources has been widely accepted by New Testament scholars (and justifiably so, it seems to me).

A second factor (in addition to form criticism) that has led to our awareness that the Gospels are not mere compilations of literary sources is a recognition that the Synoptics are *distinctive theological works*. Each bears indisputable evidence of intentional and studied arrangement. None of the Gospels is a simple chronicle of the words and deeds of Jesus; instead, all of them manifest peculiar theological and doctrinal interests.

The assertion that the first three Gospels are "confessions of faith" or theological works is commonplace in New Testament studies today. Their theological nature has been made evident by votaries of redaction criticism.[58] However, if R. H. Lightfoot knew whereof he spoke, this insight (an assumption of New Testament studies today) was not widely accepted in English theological circles at the time he delivered his Bampton Lectures (that is, in 1935, the year of publication of *The Parables of the Kingdom*). Indeed, these lectures by Lightfoot had as their thesis the then-novel contention that the Gospels *were theological documents*.[59] Recognition of the theological overtones of the Synoptics was first emphasized in Ger-

---

[57]R. H. Lightfoot, *History and Interpretation in the Gospels* (London: Hodder & Stoughton, 1935) xvi. The antipathy with which form criticism was greeted in English theological circles of the mid-1930s was also interestingly discussed by D. E. Nineham on page x of his "Introductory Memoir" in D. E. Nineham, ed., *Studies in the Gospels* (Oxford: Basil Blackwell, 1957). To the point also is a remark by T. A. Roberts: with regard to Professor Dodd's *History and the Gospels* (1938), Roberts stated that "At this time Dodd seems typical of a substantial body of English theologians who, while not exactly fighting shy of form criticism, never gave the new methodology more than qualified support." (T. A. Roberts, *History and Christian Apologetic* [London: S.P.C.K., 1960] 55.)

[58]Redaction criticism per se is not discussed in this chapter. There is a presupposing of the approach and content of works such as Hans Conzelmann, *The Theology of St. Luke*, trans. G. Buswell (New York: Harper & Row, 1960). The most readable introduction to *Redaktiongeschichte* is the late Norman Perrin's *What Is Redaction Criticism?* (Philadelphia: Fortress Press, 1969).

[59]Lightfoot, *History and Interpretation in the Gospels*, xii-xiii, 16-26, 57-96, 208-209.

many by scholars like Wrede with his renowned theory of the messianic secret. Writing concerning the tendencies of German scholarship in relationship to Mark, Lightfoot declared, "There is an increasing tendency to find interpretation continually present in a book which most of us were taught to regard as almost exclusively historical."[60] It can be said with equal force that this characteristic of interpretation is true of Matthew and Luke. In other words, biblical scholarship has come to see that all the Synoptics bear the ideological fingerprints of the men who wrote them.

Awareness that authorial creativity and theology permeate the Synoptics is a comparatively recent emphasis; it is an awareness that has come into its own *since* the creative days of source criticism. However, a recognition that the Gospels are theological documents bearing the imprint of their authors has a bearing upon our understanding of their literary interrelationship. Again, as in the case of form criticism, *it makes possible the viewing of the synoptic data in a new light.* If parallel pericopes are found in Matthew and Luke with similar though not identical wording and syntax, it does not at all follow (as source critics once conjectured) that both must be dependent upon a common literary source. Rather, allowance must be made for the *Synoptists' creative handling* of parallel versions (whether written or oral) of the same event.

The parallel accounts of the Lamp and Bushel serve to illustrate this insight. Appearing in different contexts in Matthew and Luke (Matthew 5:14-16, Luke 11:33), the two accounts have a considerable variance of both wording and syntax. The account in Matthew presupposes a simple Palestinian one-room home, whereas the Lukan account presupposes a house of Greco-Roman design. Furthermore, the application of the parable in Matthew differs from the application in Luke.[61] Yet in spite of all these dissimilarities of wording, syntax, context, and content, Streeter and Dodd both assigned the saying to Q from whence (so they argued) it was derived by Matthew and Luke. Instead of being ascribed to a hypothetical lost document, the divergent forms of the Lamp and Bushel logion can more log-

---

[60]Ibid., 57.

[61]The application of the lamp saying in Matthew concerns paradigmatic Christian discipleship ("Let your light so shine before men that they may see your good works and give glory to your Father who is in heaven"); in Luke the lamp saying is associated with the eye ("The lamp of your body is the eye. When your eyes are sound, you have light for your whole body").

ically be explained as due to the Synoptists' own creative molding and fashioning of oral and written traditions that were at their disposal. The authors of the Gospels were masters of the material they employed, not vice versa.

In his article "On Dispensing with Q," Farrer observed that "if we are not to be Streeterians, it will not be because Dr. Streeter reasoned falsely, but because the premises from which he reasoned are no longer ours."[62] The basic premise of the Streeterian approach to source analysis was that a direct literary relationship existed between prior sources and the Synoptics. Now that form criticism and a recognition of the theological distinctiveness of each of the Synoptics are a part of the heritage of New Testament studies, it is impossible any longer to accept as valid the basic premise from which the source critics approached the synoptic data.

Perhaps the sensible posture to assume at the present time toward synoptic source analysis is, to use Austin Farrer's expression, a "decent agnosticism." The problems involved have not been satisfactorily solved, and (despite the Griesbach revival) there has not yet emerged a new critical orthodoxy to replace the traditional view of synoptic sources that dominated the first half of the present century.

III. The Resultant Methodological Error

The preceding excursus on the Two-Document Hypothesis's dethroning has been necessary in order to suggest that a methodological error lies at the heart of *The Parables of the Kingdom*. Dodd, as previously observed, limited his discussion of the Kingdom to data in Mark and Q. He justified and commended this eclectic approach on the basis that Mark and Q contained the earliest traditions of the teaching of Jesus. Synoptic data outside Mark and Q (except when congenial with Dodd's conception of the Kingdom) were ignored. To express the matter another way, Professor Dodd gave "hermeneutical weight" to the Two-Document Hypothesis. His interpretation ("realized eschatology") was molded by a particular literary theory (the Two-Document Hypothesis). But to the point—in view of the pluralism and disarray prevailing today in synoptic source analysis—is a remark made by Albert C. Outler at the 1970 Pittsburgh Festival of the

---

[62]Farrer, "On Dispensing with Q," 55-56.

Gospels. With reference to current research on the synoptic problem, Professor Outler observed,

> Professor Fitzmyer's calm allowance that "the problem is practically insoluble," seems modest enough—in view of the paucity of controllable data and the conjectural character of *all* the hypotheses involved. His conclusion to stand by the *status quo ante* until something better comes along—is also at least allowable. But what will *not* follow from this (nor does Professor Fitzmyer suggest it should) is that you can then hang much hermeneutical weight on any of the various hypotheses—neither the two-source theory nor any of the others until the problem can be reexamined in new terms.[63]

Professor Outler's point concerning "hermeneutical weight" is well taken, and my contention is that Professor Dodd's assigning of *hermeneutical weight* to the Two-Document Hypothesis was a methodological mistake. Professor Dodd's policy of heeding *only* synoptic data in *Mark and Q* and of excluding all synoptic data *not in Mark and Q* is not justifiable.

Dodd's aversion to the eschatology of the primitive Christian community is well known. That for him Mark and Q were "less apocalyptic" than the rest of the synoptic material is not surprising.[64] Whether Mark and Q are *in fact* "less apocalyptic" is a questionable judgment. However, because of Dodd's aversion to apocalyptic eschatology, it is tempting to suppose that the purpose for his restricting synoptic evidence to Mark and Q was to excise futuristic references to the Kingdom (that is, references to the Kingdom as a future hope). This observation is made by Dodd's critics, and to a certain extent it may be true. But just as important for Dodd as expunging futuristic references was the excising of synoptic evidence wherein the Kingdom is presented as a place, as a realm in time and space. To Dodd the Kingdom was an abstract power operative in Jesus' ministry. Obviously, statements that speak of people sitting at table, drinking wine, eating bread, and observing Passover in the Kingdom are not accordant with this abstract conception. *Practically all synoptic evidence presenting the Kingdom in concrete details as a place occurs outside of Mark and Q*. Thus

---

[63]This statement appears on p. ix of the introduction to William R. Farmer, ed., *New Synoptic Studies: The Cambridge Gospel Conference and Beyond* (Macon GA: Mercer University Press, 1983).

[64]Dodd, *The Parables of the Kingdom*, 95, 164.

it is difficult to resist the suspicion that another motive for Dodd's Mark-Q circumscription was the expunging of all synoptic data antithetical to his abstract understanding of the Kingdom as "reign" or "power."

Let us bring this chapter to a close with a quotation from *The Peril of Modernizing Jesus* by Henry Cadbury.

> The apocalyptic element in the Gospels has been frequently laid almost exclusively to the account of the evangelists, not because there is any real evidence that Jesus did not share it, but mainly because it is uncongenial to the present-day critic. . . . The contrast in scholarly analysis of gospel material, between what is postulated as the original and the secondary, often corresponds with suspicious accuracy to the contrast between modern preferences and modern aversions.[65]

Critics divide the Gospels into sources and strata in order to select what peculiarly appeals to them. The Gospels know no such lines of demarcation. Thus, because of the disintegration of both the Marcan hypothesis and the Q hypothesis, the "darling dogma"[66] of New Testament critics, I suggest that the Mark-Q circumscription of evidence found in *The Parables of the Kingdom* is an invalid circumscription. Rather, *all synoptic data* are relevant in any attempt to understand the meaning of the Kingdom of God in Jesus' thought. In the next chapter attention will be given to the whole range of synoptic data concerning the Kingdom. The argument will be advanced that Jesus spoke of the Kingdom primarily as a place (comparable to a city or territory) and not as an exorcistic power (as Professor Dodd suggested).

Appended Note
Q—A Document or a Stratum?

The discussion in this chapter of Dodd's utilization of Q has presupposed throughout that Q was for Professor Dodd a literary document used by both Matthew and Luke. In at least one place in *The Parables of the Kingdom,* however, Q was referred to not as a document but as a stratum. Dodd cautiously observed that because the reconstruction of Q is problematical "it seems best to use the symbol for the *stratum* of the First and

---

[65]Henry J. Cadbury, *The Peril of Modernizing Jesus* (New York, 1937) 26-27.

[66]E. W. Lummis, "A Case Against Q," *Hibbert Journal* 24 (July 1926): 755.

Third Gospels in which they agree together but do not seem to depend on Mark as a source."[67] Both C. K. Barrett and Marion Hostetler[68] have cited this statement as proof that for Dodd Q was not a document but a designation for the common non-Markan material in Matthew and Luke.

Unfortunately (as the next chapter will demonstrate) terminological consistency was not one of Dodd's virtues. The observation just cited, that Q is not a document but a stratum, is anomalous, for there are scores of statements in *The Parables of the Kingdom* that indicate that for Dodd Q was a literary document. Otherwise, how could he have written concerning the *compiler* of Q,[69] or of Q originating either from Palestine or Syria,[70] or of Luke conflating Q with Mark,[71] or of Matthew conflating Q with the Second Gospel,[72] or of Matthew and Luke finding the parable of salt in a common source independent of Mark?[73] His conception of Q as a literary source can also be seen in his observations that a "verbally identical" passage in Matthew and Luke belonged "to the common source,"[74] that "Q is admittedly a compilation of originally independent sayings,"[75] and that Matthew 10:34-36 and its Lukan parallel both came from a "common written source, even though the wording differs considerably."[76]

Thus Dodd, like Streeter,[77] inconsistently used the symbol Q to designate both (a) the non-Markan material common to Matthew and Luke and (b) the presumed literary source of such material. But the references to Q as a document far outnumber the one cautious reference to it as a stratum. Therefore, a student of Dodd's thought is justified in concluding that for Dodd Q was a *literary source* used by Matthew and Luke.

---

[67]Dodd, *The Parables of the Kingdom*, 39.

[68]Barrett, "Q: A Re-examination," 320. Hostetler, "Study of the Synoptic Problem," 27.

[69]Dodd, *The Parables of the Kingdom*, 69.

[70]Ibid., 41.

[71]Ibid., 143.

[72]Ibid., 189.

[73]Ibid., 139.

[74]Ibid., 167.

[75]Ibid., 87.

[76]Ibid., 68.

[77]Hostetler, "Study of the Synoptic Problem," 50.

CHAPTER
• 3 •

A Comparison of the Use of *Basileia* in the Writings of Dodd and in the Synoptic Gospels

The previous chapter dealt with the erosion of confidence in the Two-Document Hypothesis as one reason for the necessity of rethinking realized eschatology. In this chapter we will continue our rethinking of realized eschatology by considering two additional issues. In the latter part of this chapter, I will explore Jesus' conception of the Kingdom as a *place*. That Jesus conceived of the Kingdom as a realm—comparable to a territory or to a city—becomes obvious when attention is given to *all* synoptic data (not just to selected, slanted data from Mark and Q). This insight is significant; it is contrary to Professor Dodd's conception of the Kingdom (βασιλεία, *basileia*) as a curative power operative in Jesus' exorcisms.

In the first part of this chapter, however, I want to deal with another issue: *Professor Dodd's slippery use of language*. Among New Testament scholars C. H. Dodd was a giant. Yet even a giant can have weaknesses. Having read most of the books and journal articles that came from his pen, I am convinced that Professor Dodd's primary foible as a theologian was his failure to use terminology with consistency. Nowhere can this weakness be seen more clearly than in the manifold meanings he gave to *basileia* (Kingdom). The intention of the following discussion is to demonstrate how Professor Dodd used *basileia* in a bewildering variety of senses. This semantic ambiguity obviously weakens his discussion of what the Kingdom of God means.

I. The Ambiguity of *Basileia* in the Writings of C. H. Dodd

Largely through Gustaf Dalman's classic *Die Worte Jesu* the attention of scholars was drawn to the insight that *basileia* in the similar phrases "Kingdom of God" and "Kingdom of Heaven" was a rendering of the Aramaic word *malkuth* (מַלְכוּת). This Aramaic word usually means "Kingdom" in the sense of a territory ruled by a king. But, as Dalman pointed out, it can also have an abstract force signifying "reign" or "kingship."

A cursory reading of *The Parables of the Kingdom* reveals that Professor Dodd accepted without reservation this abstract signification suggested by Dalman. Footnoting Dalman as his authority, Dodd wrote,

> But there can be no doubt that the expression before us represents an Aramaic phrase well-established in Jewish usage, "The *malkuth* of Heaven." *Malkuth,* like other substantives of the same formation, is properly an abstract noun, meaning "kingship," "kingly rule," "reign," or "sovereignty." The expression "the *malkuth* of God" connotes the fact that God reigns as King. In sense, though not in grammatical form, the substantive conception in the phrase "the Kingdom of God" is the idea of God, and the term "kingdom" indicates that specific aspect, attribute or activity of God, in which He is revealed as King or sovereign Lord of His people, or of the universe which He created.[1]

Thus, throughout *The Parables of the Kingdom* the term *basileia* was given an abstract signification. It was variously defined as meaning "sov-

---

[1] C. H. Dodd, *The Parables of the Kingdom* (London: James Nisbet and Company, 1935) 34-35 (21 in 1961 rev. ed.). Much to the point, however, is an observation by Cecil John Cadoux on page 113 of *The Historic Mission of Jesus* (London: Lutterworth Press, 1941): "Our authorities tell us that in Jewish literature at least, the phrase, 'the Kingdom of God' is always used in an intensive sense, never extensively of the group, realm, or territory over which God reigns. However that may be, it is palpable that in the teaching of Jesus the term often has an extensive connotation. Sayings in which mention is made of 'entering' the Kingdom, being 'greatest' or 'least' in it, seeing the Patriarchs in it (Lk. xiii.28-Mt. viii. 11 Q), shining out in it (Mt. xiii. 43 M), being gathered out of it (Mt. xiii. 41 M), or having it closed against one by others (Mt. xxiii. 13), cannot be naturally interpreted if 'the kingdom' must always mean only the royal sovereignty of God. The mention of such sovereignty often brings to mind at once the thought of those over whom it is exercised. In passages in which that thought is to the fore, 'the Kingdom' will be quite a good English equivalent of the Greek."

ereignty,"[2] "kingship,"[3] "kingly rule,"[4] "the sovereign power of God."[5] Furthermore, Dodd argued that this abstract *basileia* was manifest in Jesus' demon exorcisms. In his exegesis of Matthew 12:28, the proof text par excellence of realized eschatology, he wrote,

> But Jesus says, "If I, by the finger of God, cast out demons, then the Kingdom of God has come upon you." Something has happened, which has not happened before, and which means that the sovereign power of God has come into effective operation. It is not a matter of having God for your King in the sense that you obey His commandments: *it is a matter of being confronted with the power of God at work in the world. In other words, the "eschatological" Kingdom of God is proclaimed as a present fact,* which men must recognize, whether by their actions they accept or reject it.[6]

To express the matter another way, *basileia* in the sense of the "sovereign power of God" was the agent by which Jesus expelled demons. Equating demon exorcism (or the overcoming of Satan's kingdom) with the *basileia's* arrival, Professor Dodd wrote,

> In the "Q" context from which the words "the Kingdom of God has come upon you" have been quoted, the exorcisms performed by Jesus are treated as a sign that the kingdom of Satan has been overcome. As in the *Testament of Dan,* this is equivalent to the coming of the kingdom of God. But here the coming has not waited until Israel should repent. In some way the Kingdom of God has come with Jesus himself.[7]

The next chapter will belabor the point that interpreting *basileia* as a curative-exorcistic power has become widely accepted in Anglo-American biblical studies. The validity of this interpretation will be questioned, and the argument will be made that Professor Dodd confused *basileia* with such concepts as *pneuma* (πνεῦμα) and *dunamis* (δύναμις). Be that as it may, over and over again in *The Parables of the Kingdom* the contention

---

[2]Dodd, *The Parables of the Kingdom,* 46.

[3]Ibid., 36-38.

[4]Ibid., 37-38.

[5]Ibid., 44.

[6]Ibid.; italics added (29 in 1961 rev. ed.).

[7]Ibid., 45 (1961 rev. ed., 30).

is made that in synoptic thought the Kingdom arrived with Jesus. "In some way the Kingdom of God has come with Jesus himself."[8] To this contention Dodd originally gave the designation "realized eschatology,"[9] and as observed in the opening chapter, this "Kingdom version" of realized eschatology has exerted a pervasive influence in Anglo-American theological discussions.

Unfortunately, however, in *The Parables of the Kingdom*, Dodd did not consistently adhere to this demon-exorcising conception of *basileia* that has just been noted. Numerous readings of *The Parables of the Kingdom* have convinced me that Dodd (in a subtle, almost imperceptible way) engaged in paraphrasing eisegesis and gave *basileia* unwarranted extensions of meaning wherein it became a *term inclusive of historical events*. From a semantic-hermeneutical standpoint this pliable, expansive use of *basileia* eludes precise analysis. This expansive use can more easily be illustrated than defined. However, I have in mind Professor Dodd's use of *basileia* as an encompassing term to include, on one hand, *the series of events that constituted Jesus' ministry* and, on the other hand, *the experiences of Jesus' early followers*. Moreover, there is still another extension of meaning wherein the Kingdom was presented by Dodd as a *potentiality or possibility for people of all time*. Illustrations or examples will now be given of these diverse uses of "Kingdom"—uses that manifestly cannot be reconciled with the abstract conception of *basileia* as a demon-exorcising power operative in Jesus' life. It is important to note that Dodd did *not* cite biblical evidence to justify these additional, diverse uses of *basileia*. The reason for this failure to cite supporting biblical data is obvious. There is none.

For example, on occasion Dodd used the term *Kingdom* to encompass *the complex of events that composed Jesus' ministry*. Illustrative of this use is the following citation:

---

[8] Ibid., 45, 47, 63, 74, 75, 76, 78, 79, 113, 114.

[9] Ibid., 51. The chief cornerstone in the structure of realized eschatology (as presented in *The Parables of the Kingdom*) is an abstract understanding of *basileia*. Subsequently in this chapter it will be argued that it is an oversimplification of the Gospel data to suggest that *basileia* in the Synoptics means primarily "reign" or "power" or "sovereignty." There are numerous passages in the Gospels where it is palpable that *kingdom* is *not* used in an *abstract* but in a *concrete sense*. Many of these passages did not come within Dodd's purview, however, because they appear outside Mark and Q.

As we have seen, the coming of the Kingdom of God is in the teaching of Jesus not a momentary event, but a complex of interrelated events including His own ministry, His death, and what follows, all conceived as forming a unity.[10]

Or consider the following quotations I have selected at random from *The Parables of the Kingdom:*

> The parables of growth, then, are susceptible of a natural interpretation which makes them into a commentary on the actual situation during the ministry of Jesus, in its character as the coming of the Kingdom of God in history.[11]
>
> For eternal life is the ultimate issue of *the coming of the Kingdom of God, and this coming is manifested in the series of historical events which unfolds itself in the ministry of Jesus.*[12]
>
> The coming of the Son of Man is the coming of the Kingdom of God.[13]

As these just-cited quotations indicate, the conception of *basileia* as a curative power that made possible Jesus' exorcisms was quietly abandoned, and Dodd argued that historical events in the life of Jesus somehow embodied or expressed the Kingdom of God. Admittedly this use of *basileia* is not perspicuous. But neither is Professor Dodd's use of "Kingdom" to encompass events *in the lives both of Jesus' followers and the Jewish people who rejected Jesus.* Consider the following remark by Professor Dodd.

---

[10]Ibid., 185.

[11]Ibid., 193.

[12]Ibid., 50-51; italics added.

[13]Ibid., 114. This identification of the Kingdom and the coming of the son of Man is contradicted on p. 107 of *The Parables of the Kingdom;* for here Dodd distinguished the Kingdom and the Son of Man in these words, "But Jesus declares that this ultimate, the Kingdom of God, has come into history, and He takes upon himself the 'eschatological' role of 'Son of Man.' The absolute, the 'wholly other,' has entered into time and space. And as the Kingdom of God has come and the Son of Man has come, so also judgment and blessedness have come into human experience."

Thus both the facts of the life of Jesus, and the events which he foretells within the historical order, are "eschatological" events for they fall within the coming of the Kingdom of God.[14]

A reading of *The Parables of the Kingdom* reveals that by "events which he foretells within the historical order" Professor Dodd was referring to Jesus' prophecy of his own violent death, the persecution of his followers, and the disaster the Jewish people and their temple met at the hands of the Romans. Thus Jesus' crucifixion, early Christian persecution, and the Jewish revolt of A.D. 70 are viewed by Dodd as expressing the Kingdom of God. A similar thought is found in the following quotation:

> It is in this context that the parables of the Kingdom of God must be placed. They use all the resources of dramatic illustration to help men to see that in the events before their eyes—in the miracles of Jesus, His appeal to men and its results, the blessedness that comes to those who follow Him, and the hardening of those who reject Him; in the tragic conflict of the Cross, and the tribulation of the disciples; in the fateful choice before the Jewish people, and the disasters that threaten—God is confronting them in His Kingdom.[15]

Or commenting on the parable of the Bridegroom and Wedding Guests in Mark 2:18-20, Dodd observed,

> If the parable meant, as I have suggested, that the disciples enjoy pure happiness because they are "in the Kingdom of God," then it is impossible to suppose that the time for rejoicing will soon pass, and the time for fasting return; for the Kingdom of God endures.[16]

The preceding citations illustrate how Dodd, in a not-too-clear manner, reasoned that the Kingdom was embodied in events in the lives of Jesus' contemporaries. The abandonment of an abstract understanding of *basileia* (as an exorcising power) is likewise seen in his argument that out-

---

[14]Ibid., 107. By the phrase "events which he foretells within the historical order" Dodd meant Jesus' prophecy of his own violent death, the persecution of his followers, and the disaster the Jewish people and their temple met at the hands of the Romans (see *The Parables of the Kingdom*, 66-67).

[15]Ibid., 197-98.

[16]Ibid., 116.

casts can "be seen flocking into the Kingdom of God,"[17] and in his argument that *the Kingdom is a possibility for people of all time.* This is expressed in the peroration of the book wherein Dodd declared,

> We have, it appears, no warrant in the teaching of Jesus for affirming that the long cycles of history will lead inevitably to a millennial "Kingdom Come" on earth. But we have warrant for affirming that God comes to meet us in history, and sets before us the open but narrow door into His Kingdom. To accept His Kingdom and to enter in brings blessedness, because the best conceivable thing is that we should be in obedience to the will of God.[18]

Perhaps Dodd's paralleling of the Kingdom of God with "true religion"[19] was to be understood as a kind of *lapsus linguae,* and at least once Dodd wrote that the "Kingdom of God is, in a familiar figure, a feast of the blessed."[20] Thus in *The Parables of the Kingdom* the reader is variously informed that *kingdom* means reign, kingship, kingly rule, sovereignty, true religion, a feast of the blessed, a timeless reality,[21] the power and glory of the blessed God,[22] the ultimate good and the final power in the universe,[23] and the coming of the Son of Man.[24] The reader is also informed that the Kingdom is something that endures forever, into which men may enter, and that it is embodied in the ministry of Jesus, the cross, demon exorcism, the hardening of those who reject Jesus, the persecution of Jesus' disciples, the Roman invasion of Palestine, and the destruction of the Jewish temple.

The cataloguing of diverse meanings given *basileia* in *The Parables of the Kingdom* by no means exhausts the definitions of *basileia* that can be found in Dodd's writings. Reflecting the Platonic frame of reference

---

[17]Ibid., 199.

[18]Ibid., 209 (169 in 1961 rev. ed.).

[19]Ibid., 16.

[20]Ibid., 116.

[21]Ibid., 80.

[22]Ibid.

[23]Ibid., 208.

[24]Ibid., 172.

from which he approached New Testament studies, Dodd in *The Apostolic Preaching and Its Developments* defined the Kingdom as "pure reality." The Kingdom of God is "righteousness, peace, and joy; that is, it is the pure reality which we partly apprehend in the most exalted moments of our human experience in time."[25] But in the same year (1936) that Dodd defined the Kingdom as "pure reality," he was also contending in *The Expository Times* that the Kingdom's coming was to be equated with Pentecost.[26]

There are places in Dodd's writings where he came close to identifying the Kingdom with the Church (the Augustinian interpretation) or with the ideal moral system (the interpretation popularized by the social gospel movement). Consider the following quotations from Dodd's *History and the Gospel:*

> As the destruction of Jerusalem is the historical embodiment of the Kingdom as judgment, so the *koinonia* of the Church is the historical embodiment of the Kingdom of God as the gift of eternal life. . . . The coming of the Kingdom of God, which revealed itself as judgment in the rejection of Israel, revealed itself as mercy in Christ's return to his undeserving disciples, and in creating out of them the fellowship of the Church as an historical society.[27]

With reference to Jesus' ethical teaching Dodd wrote, "It is the absolute ethic of the Kingdom of God, the moral principles of a new order of life."[28] In *The Kingdom of God and History,* published in 1938, Professor Dodd asserted that the Kingdom

> came with Jesus Christ, and its coming was perceived to be eternal in its quality. That eternal quality is manifested in time by the continuous life of the Church, centered in sacrament. . . . It comes with judgment upon

---

[25] C. H. Dodd, *The Apostolic Preaching and Its Developments* (London: Hodder & Stoughton, 1936; New York: Harper and Row, 1964) 84.

[26] C. H. Dodd, "The Kingdom of God Has Come," *Expository Times* 48 (December 1936): 142.

[27] C. H. Dodd, *History and the Gospel* (London: James Nisbet and Company, 1938) 138, 175.

[28] Ibid., 125.

the evil of the world, and the Church always knows that "it is time for judgment to begin with the House of God."[29]

Or, in *The Bible and Its Background,* in regard to Matthew's Gospel, he wrote that

> Its author must have been an experienced teacher, for nothing could be more admirably adapted to a teacher's use. He has made the scattered sayings into long discourses like the Sermon on the Mount, built up with architectural skill. His picture of Jesus brings out another side from that of Mark. Here Christ is the immortal King who gives the Laws of the Kingdom of God.[30]

Thus in writings published between 1930 and 1940, the decade during which he advanced his hypothesis of realized eschatology, Dodd argued that *Kingdom* either means, suggests, is embodied in, or is to be equated with:

1. reign, sovereignty, kingship, kingly rule, *malkuth*
2. the absolute
3. the "wholly other"
4. the ultimate
5. a new order of life
6. true religion
7. a feast of the blessed
8. a timeless reality
9. the power and glory of the blessed God
10. the ultimate good and final power in the universe
11. the coming of the Son of Man
12. the ministry of Jesus (particularly demon exorcisms)
13. the cross
14. the hardening of those who reject Jesus
15. the tribulation of the disciples of Christ
16. the Roman invasion of Palestine
17. the destruction of the Jewish temple
18. righteousness, peace, and joy

---

[29] C. H. Dodd, *The Kingdom of God and History* (London: George Allen and Unwin, 1938) 35.

[30] C. H. Dodd, *The Bible and Its Background* (London: George Allen and Unwin, 1931) 71.

19. the pure reality we partly apprehend in the most exalted moments of our human experience in time
20. Pentecost
21. the destruction of Jerusalem
22. the *koinonia* of the Church
23. the rejection of Israel
24. the creation of the fellowship of the Church as a historical society and the continuous life of the Church centered in the Sacrament
25. the post-Resurrection appearances of Jesus
26. a community with laws and an absolute ethic
27. judgment upon the evil of the world
28. Christ's return to His undeserving disciples

To reconcile these diverse conceptions would tax the wits of the most adroit sophist. In the writings of Professor Dodd, the Kingdom of God is semantic putty, a concept pulled and pushed in all directions.

In presenting these diverse conceptions Dodd cited biblical evidence to support *only one of them,* that is, the conception of the Kingdom as "reign" or "power." This is the conception that dominates *The Parables of the Kingdom.* An examination of the tenuous data (Matthew 11:2-6, 12-13; 12:28, 41; 13:16-17; Mark 1:14-15; and Lukan parallels) used by Dodd to argue that the Kingdom should be understood abstractly as "reign" or "power" will be considered in the next chapter.

Having argued that Professor Dodd was appallingly slippery in his use of language (assigning to *Kingdom* multiple referents and thereby committing the fallacy of equivocation), I want to level the same criticism against the mediating theologians (that is, those apologists who desire to synthesize Schweitzer with Dodd and who try to argue that the Kingdom was *both present and future in Jesus' thinking*). As I have previously suggested, few hermeneutical theories are more widely accepted today than the theory that the historical Jesus taught that the Kingdom of God was both present and future. Proponents of this theory always use the term *Kingdom* in the singular (not the plural). They do not say, "The Kingdoms were present and future." Rather they assert, "The Kingdom was present and future." This singular usage suggests that *Kingdom* has *one referent,* and that the *same referent* was both present and future. At this point the mediating theologians play a trick upon themselves and upon others. They are guilty of an unrecognized language error (that is, *a shift in referents*). They fail to perceive that consistent eschatologists and realized eschatologists define the Kingdom of God *differently*. Both use the term *Kingdom* but they use *different referents*. For consistent eschatologists, the referent for Kingdom was the imminent Golden Age of Jewish eschatological hopes; for realized eschatologists its referent was the curative, exorcistic power operative in Jesus. To consistent eschatologists the Kingdom is a place; to realized eschatologists the Kingdom is a power.

Obviously a curative, exorcistic power is not the same as a spatial Golden Age. Thus the mediating theologians make an unwarranted move when they try to synthesize or to combine these ideas. They are not justified in reasoning, "Thanks to Schweitzer and to Dodd we have come to see that the Kingdom (singular) was both present and future." Rather (if they desire to be consistent) the mediating theologians should say, "Thanks to Schweitzer and to Dodd we have come to see that in the New Testament the term *Kingdom* has two different denotations: (1) a healing exorcistic power and (2) the Golden Age of eschatological expectations."

Once you and I recognize that Kingdom is assigned two different referents, we are then in a position to perceive that for years the mediating theologians have been allowed to get away with an unjustifiable "bait-and-switch" maneuver. They "bait" us with one conception of the Kingdom, that is, the conception of the Kingdom as a curative power that was present in Jesus. The mediating theologians (appealing to Matthew 12:28, Luke 11:20) look us in the eye and declare, "The Kingdom was present in Jesus' exorcisms." While still looking us in the eye and mesmerizing us with discussions on how *basileia* is to be understood in terms of *malkuth,* the mediating theologians go one step further and affirm, "And by the way, this Kingdom we have told you was present was also future." But in this future claim they abandon their bait's referent to the Kingdom (a curative power) and switch to an entirely different referent (the eschatological interpretation found in Johannes Weiss and Albert Schweitzer). This bait-and-switch maneuver is, I contend, a deceiving manipulation of language. The mediating theologians who use this bait-and-switch maneuver are like crafty Jacob about whom we read in Genesis. Jacob tried to combine his voice and Esau's hands. Yet Jacob's voice and Esau's hands did not belong together. Similarly, the mediating theologians try to combine Dodd's view of the Kingdom with Schweitzer's view of the Kingdom. But, like Jacob's voice and Esau's hands, these two views do not belong together; indeed, they contradict each other and cannot be juxtaposed as mediating theologians attempt to do.

Moreover, having conceded that a futuristic conception of the Kingdom is present in Jesus' teachings, the mediating theologians quietly abandon this awkward conception, allowing it to fade into oblivion. They subsequently switch back to the bait and focus on the conception of the Kingdom as a curative power present in Jesus' ministry. They *assume* this curative power is still present and is somehow operative within the Church. Curiously they fail to cite illustrations of contemporary healings and exorcisms that would prove that the *basileia* is in fact operative in our day.

II. The Kingdom in the Synoptics: A Realm or Place

Having given attention to the diverse ways in which Professor Dodd defined the Kingdom, I now want us to confront this question: *How did Jesus use the phrase "Kingdom of God"*? What did he mean by this expression? In grappling with this question, I propose we return to the Two-Document Hypothesis issue that was discussed in the preceding chapter. In this discussion the point was belabored that Professor Dodd *used only Mark and Q material* in his interpretation of the Kingdom. He ignored data outside Mark and Q. Yet, if *all synoptic data* are heeded, an irresistible conclusion emerges: Jesus used the expression "Kingdom of God" primarily in a *spatial sense*.[31] Over one hundred statements occur in the synoptics wherein the term *Kingdom (basileia)* is used. The majority of these statements correlate with the view that for Jesus the Kingdom was a *realm* in time and space. In Jesus' thinking the Kingdom was not a curative-exorcistic "power" as realized eschatologists suggest. Rather, it was a *place* that was the antithesis of hell and that could be bodily entered. This spatial interpretation is not new; it was persuasively presented by Johannes Weiss in his *Die Predigt Jesu vom Reiche Gottes* (1892), a book to which Pro-

---

[31]There are several instances in the Synoptics where βασιλεία is used but not in reference to the Kingdom of God (Matthew 4:8; Mark 3:24 with parallels in Matthew 12:25 and Luke 11:17; Mark 6:23; Mark 13:8 with parallels in Matthew 24:7 and Luke 21:10). It would be instructive to note if in these instances βασιλεία is used in an abstract or concrete sense. That βασιλεία is not used as an abstract noun, but rather as a concrete one, is obvious from the fact that it is paralleled with such concrete words as οἰκία, πόλις, and ἔθνος. The concrete overtones of βασιλεία in Matthew 4:8 (parallel in Luke 4:5) and Mark 6:23 are obvious. That in these instances βασιλεία has a concrete significance points to the possibility that βασιλεία in the phrase βασιλεία τοῦ θεοῦ has a similar concrete significance.

fessor Dodd never refers. Further elaboration of this territorial view was provided by scholars like Albert Schweitzer. Yet Weiss's view, never disproven, is curiously ignored by many Anglo-American exegetes. This ignoring of Weiss's view, however, does not invalidate it.

In order to understand why Johannes Weiss reasoned as he did, let us survey *what Jesus taught* about the Kingdom of God. In our survey I will not cite *every* statement Jesus made concerning the Kingdom (this I have done in Appendix I wherein all synoptic verses containing the word *Kingdom* are cited in full). Instead, I will quote representative statements. Nowhere—regretfully—among Jesus' sayings is there a definition of the Kingdom of God.[32] Evidently the synoptists *assumed* their readers knew what this phrase meant. Nor is there reason to believe they recorded every detail of Jesus' teachings. Indeed, the recorded sayings probably represent only a fragment of Jesus' instruction. Thus questions arise in our minds for which we have no answers. *Where* did Jesus expect the Kingdom to come? Did he expect it to come in Galilee? Or perhaps at Jerusalem? *How* did Jesus expect the Kingdom to come? Did he expect it to come down out of heaven on clouds of glory? To answer these questions is impossible. But we do have a number of Jesus' Kingdom pronouncements, and these pronouncements can be categorized. When categorized, these pronouncements enable us to profile (in an incomplete and indistinct manner) Jesus' conception of the Kingdom of God. A number of these pronouncements deal with eating and drinking in the Kingdom. We will begin our survey with these food and drink sayings. This survey may appear tedious, but it is necessary to help us grasp what the historical Jesus actually taught so we will not be charmed into swallowing "modern, sophisticated" interpretations of the Kingdom that have no basis in Jesus' pronouncements.

After we have surveyed what Jesus said about the Kingdom, we will then confront this hermeneutical question: What interpretive theory best "explains" the observations Jesus made about the Kingdom? How can his Kingdom sayings be made to "make sense" to the modern mind?

---

[32]Charles Guignebert, *Jesus,* trans. S. H. Hooke (New York: University Books, 1956) 330; Martin Dibelius, *Jesus,* trans. Charles B. Hendrick and Frederick C. Grant (Philadelphia: Westminster Press, 1939) 66: "Any attempt to interpret the individual sayings of Jesus about the Kingdom must be preceded by a recognition of the fact that *Jesus never specifically interpreted the expression 'Kingdom of God.'* "

1. The Kingdom as a Place of Eating and Drinking

Statements that affirm that people will sit at tables, eat, and drink wine point in the direction of the Kingdom as a place. Consider, for example, the discussion of the Narrow Door in Luke.

> Strive to enter by the narrow door; for many, I tell you, will seek to enter and will not be able. When once the householder has risen up and shut the door, you will begin to stand outside and to knock at the door, saying, "Lord, open to us." He will answer you, "I do not know where you come from." Then you will begin to say, "We ate and drank in your presence, and you taught in our streets." But he will say, "I tell you, I do not know where you come from; depart from me, all you workers of iniquity!" There you will weep and gnash your teeth, when you see Abraham and Isaac and Jacob and all the prophets in the kingdom of God and yourself thrust out. And men will come from east and west, and from north and south, *and sit at table in the Kingdom of God.* (Luke 13:24-29)

Or consider the following quotations, two of which were made by Jesus in the context of the Last Supper.

> I tell you, many will come from east and west and *sit at table with Abraham, Isaac, and Jacob in the kingdom of heaven,* while the sons of the kingdom will be thrown into the outer darkness; there men will weep and gnash their teeth. (Matthew 8:11-12)

> And he took a cup, and when he had given thanks he gave it to them, saying, "Drink of it, all of you; for this is my blood of the covenant, which is poured out for many for the forgiveness of sins. I tell you *I shall not drink again of this fruit of the vine until that day when I drink it new with you in my Father's kingdom."* (Matthew 26:27-29 ‖ Mark 14:25)

> And when the hour came, he sat at table, and the apostles with him. And he said to them, *"I have earnestly desired to eat this Passover with you before I suffer; for I tell you I shall not eat it until it is fulfilled in the Kingdom of God."* (Luke 22:14-16)

> When one of those who sat at table with him heard this, he said to him, *"Blessed is he who shall eat bread in the kingdom of God!"* (Luke 14:15)

> "You are those who have continued with me in my trials; as my Father appointed a kingdom for me, so do I appoint for you that *you may eat and drink at my table in my kingdom,* and sit on thrones judging the twelve tribes of Israel." (Luke 22:28-30)

An examination of these quoted passages reveals numerous concrete features. The apostles will have the honor of eating and drinking at table with Jesus. Many will come from east and west and sit at table with Abraham, Isaac, and Jacob. Jesus anticipated eating Passover and drinking wine in the Kingdom. There is no indication he disagreed with the man who exclaimed, "Blessed is he who shall eat bread in the Kingdom of God," for it was in the context of this exclamation that Jesus delivered the well-known Banquet parable (Luke 14:16-24). Also it must be noted that in Matthew's Gospel Jesus compared the Kingdom to a marriage feast (Matthew 22:1-14). The sensory-spatial implications of these references to sitting at table, eating, and drinking wine are obvious.

2. The Kingdom as a Place with Stations of Honor

Further evidence that Jesus thought of the Kingdom as a realm is seen in the idea of different ranks or stations of honor. Consider, for example, the winsome story of the request made for the sons of Zebedee.

> Then the mother of the sons of Zebedee came up to him, with her sons, and kneeling before him she asked him for something. And he said to her, "What do you want?" She said to him, "Command that these two sons of mine may sit, one at your right hand and one at your left, in your kingdom." But Jesus answered, "You do not know what you are asking. Are you able to drink the cup that I am to drink?" They said to him, "We are able." He said to them, "You will drink my cup, but to sit at my right hand and at my left is not mine to grant, but it is for those for whom it has been prepared by my Father." (Matthew 20:20-33)

That different ranks of honor will exist in the Kingdom is suggested by the following passages:

> Whoever then relaxes one of the least of these commandments and teaches men so, shall be called least in the kingdom of heaven; but he who does them and teaches them shall be called great in the kingdom of heaven. For I tell you, unless your righteousness exceeds that of the scribes and Pharisees, you will never enter the kingdom of heaven.
> (Matthew 5:19-20)

> Truly, I say to you, among those born of women there has risen no one greater than John the Baptist; yet he who is least in the kingdom of heaven is greater than he. (Matthew 11:11 || Luke 7:20)

> At that time the disciples came to Jesus, saying, "Who is the greatest in the kingdom of heaven?" And calling to him a child, he put him in the

midst of them, and said, "Truly, I say to you, unless you turn and become like children, you will never enter the kingdom of heaven. Whoever humbles himself like this child, he is the greatest in the kingdom of heaven." (Matthew 18:1-4)

In regard to status, Jesus believed that when the Kingdom arrived his twelve disciples would rule the tribes of Israel.

"As my Father appointed a kingdom for me, so do I appoint for you that you may eat and drink at my table in my kingdom, and sit on thrones judging the twelve tribes of Israel." (Luke 22:29-30)

"Truly I say to you, in the new world, when the Son of Man shall sit on his glorious throne, you who have followed me will also sit on twelve thrones, judging the twelve tribes of Israel." (Matthew 19:28)

The strategic role the Twelve were to play in the soon-to-arrive Kingdom is the reason (so Krister Stendahl suggested) for their refusal to leave Jerusalem after Stephen's persecution. It was obligatory for them to remain in Jerusalem in order to assume the roles of tribal judges when the Kingdom arrived.

Related to different ranks or stations is the belief that scribes and eunuchs will be in the Kingdom.

And he said to them, "Therefore every scribe who has been trained for the kingdom of heaven is like a house-holder who brings out of this treasure what is new and what is old." (Matthew 13:52)

"For there are eunuchs who have been so from birth, and there are eunuchs who have been made eunuchs by men, and there are eunuchs who have made themselves eunuchs for the sake of the kingdom of heaven. He who is able to receive this, let him receive it." (Matthew 19:12)

3. The Kingdom as a Place to Be Entered Bodily and to Be Seen with the Eye

Because the Kingdom is spatial, it is possible to enter into it (like entering into a city or country). When speaking of entering the Kingdom, the Synoptists always (with the exception of Matthew 21:31) use some form of the verb εἰσέρχομαι. To overlook the spatial implications of the εἰσέρχομαι entry logia is easy. Yet it must be noted that εἰσέρχομαι is a common Greek verb used throughout the New Testament to express such actions as walking into a house or walking into a city (for example, Matthew 12:43; Mark 2:1). Consider the following entry logia that employ this verb to denote entrance into the Kingdom.

> "And if your eye causes you to sin, pluck it out; it is better for you to enter the kingdom of God with one eye than with two eyes to be thrown into hell."[33] (Mark 9:47)

> And Jesus looked around and said to his disciples, "How hard it will be for those who have riches to enter the kingdom of God!" (Mark 10:23 ‖ Luke 18:24-25)

> "For I tell you, unless your righteousness exceeds that of the scribes and Pharisees, you will never enter the kingdom of heaven."[34] (Matthew 5:20)

Other references to entering the Kingdom appear in Matthew 7:21; 18:3; 19:23-24; 21:31; 23:13; Mark 10:15, 23, 24, 25; and Luke 18:17. All these references indicate that for Jesus the Kingdom was not an abstract sovereignty; rather, it was a place or a land in which people walk, sit, eat, and drink. It is possible to be *thrown out* of the Kingdom, and Jesus anticipated the physical removal of the unrighteous.

> "There you will weep and gnash your teeth, when you see Abraham and Isaac and Jacob and all the prophets in the kingdom of God and you yourselves thrown out." (Luke 13:28)

> "I tell you, many will come from east and west and sit at table with Abraham, Isaac, and Jacob in the kingdom of heaven, while the sons of the kingdom will be thrown out into the outer darkness."[35] (Matthew 8:11-12)

The idea of being thrown out of the Kingdom is also found in Matthew 13:47-50. In all these passages the verbs βάλλω and ἐκβάλλω are used—graphic evidence that for Jesus the Kingdom was spatial.

---

[33] Note that in this verse *basileia* is paralleled with "hell."

[34] With reference to the anomalous Luke 17:21 it should be noted that in synoptic thought the *basileia* does not enter man; rather, man enters the *basileia*.

[35] With reference to the bodily expulsion of the unrighteous, note the following quotation from the parable of the Weeds: "The Son of Man will send his angels, and they will gather out of his Kingdom all causes of sin and all evildoers, and throw them into the furnace of fire; there men will weep and gnash their teeth." (Matthew 13:41-42)

The hypothesis that for Jesus the Kingdom will be a realm or land explains why the Kingdom (on its arrival) will be visible to the eye.

> "Truly, I say to you, there are some standing here who will not taste death before they see the kingdom of God come with power." (Mark 9:1)

> "Truly I say to you, there are some standing here who will not taste death before they see the son of man coming in his kingdom."[36] (Matthew 16:28 ‖ Luke 9:27)

> "There you will weep and gnash your teeth, when you see Abraham and Isaac and Jacob and all the prophets in the kingdom of God and you yourselves thrust out."[37] (Luke 13:28)

These verses obviously conceive of the Kingdom as an object of vision.

4. The Kingdom and the Satisfaction of Material Needs

Pertinent to a discussion of the Kingdom as a realm is a Sermon-on-the-Mount passage that teaches that those who live in the Kingdom will have their material needs satisfied.

> "Therefore do not be anxious, saying, 'What shall we eat?' or 'What shall we drink?' or 'What shall we wear?' For the Gentiles seek all these things; and your heavenly Father knows that you need them all. *But seek first his kingdom and his righteousness, and all these things shall be yours as well.*" (Matthew 6:31-33; italics added ‖ Luke 12:31)

The idea that in the Kingdom the need for food and clothing will be satisfied is repeated in the Lukan beatitudes.

> And he lifted up his eyes on his disciples, and said: "*Blessed are you poor, for yours in the kingdom of God. Blessed are you that hunger now,

---

[36] In Matthean thought there is no sharp distinction between the Kingdom of God and the Kingdom of the Son of man (note the parable of the Weeds in Matthew 13:24-30, 36-43).

[37] The observation made concerning Joseph of Arimathea in Mark 15:43 ("Joseph of Arimathea, a respected member of the council, who was also himself looking for the kingdom of God, took courage and went to Pilate, and asked for the body of Jesus"), with a parallel in Luke 23:51, does not speak of the kingdom as an object of vision. In these verses προσδέχομαι ("to expect," "to look for," "to wait for") is used. It is palpable, however, from the use of προσδέχομαι that in Mark 15:43 ‖ Luke 23:51 the Kingdom was conceived as a future hope.

for you shall be satisfied. Blessed are you that weep now, for you shall laugh. Blessed are you when men hate you, and when they exclude you and revile you, and cast out your name as evil, on account of the Son of man! Rejoice in that day, and leap for joy, for behold, your reward is great in heaven; for so their fathers did to the prophets.''

(Luke 6:20-23; italics added)

Because his followers would soon no longer concern themselves with food and clothing, Jesus exhorted them to live lives of holy poverty.

"Fear not, little flock, for it is your Father's good pleasure to give you the kingdom. Sell your possessions, and give alms; provide yourselves with purses that do not grow old, with a treasure in the heavens that does not fail, where no thief approaches and moth destroys. For where your treasure is, there will your heart be also."[38] (Luke 12:32-34)

5. Jesus as the Doorkeeper to the Kingdom

Another indication of the Kingdom's spatial nature is the teaching that people will enter the Kingdom through a narrow door. Jesus will be the doorkeeper and will determine who is permitted or denied entrance. That Jesus looked upon himself as the one who will allow or refuse entrance is expressed in the Sermon on the Mount in this way.

"Not every one who says to me, 'Lord, Lord,' shall enter the kingdom of heaven, but he who does the will of my Father who is in heaven. On that day many will say to me, 'Lord, Lord, did we not prophesy in your name, and cast out demons in your name, and do many mighty works in your name?' And then will I declare to them, 'I never knew you; depart from me, you evildoers.' " (Matthew 7:21-23)

The conception of entry into the Kingdom through a narrow door is found in Luke 13:22-29. To understand this pericope, one must remember that in synoptic thought "to be saved" can refer to entering the Kingdom (Mark 10:26, with parallels in Luke 18:26 and Matthew 19:25).

---

[38]The material blessings of the impending Golden Age are painted in glowing terms in Matthew's Gospel: "And everyone who has left houses or brothers or sisters or father or mother or children or lands, for my name's sake, will receive a hundredfold and inherit eternal life." (Matthew 19:29 || Luke 18:29-30)

> He went on his way through towns and villages, teaching, and journeying toward Jerusalem. And some one said to him, "Lord, will those who are saved be few?" And he said to them, "Strive to to enter by the narrow door; for many, I tell you, will seek to enter and will not be able. When once the householder has risen up and shut the door, you will begin to stand outside and to knock at the door saying, 'Lord, open to us.' He will answer you, 'I do not know where you come from.' Then you will begin to say, 'We ate and drank in your presence, and you taught in our streets.' But he will say, 'I tell you, I do not know where you come from; depart from me, all you workers of iniquity!' There you will weep and gnash your teeth, when you see Abraham and Isaac and Jacob and all the prophets in the kingdom of God and you yourselves thrust out. And men will come from east and west, and from north and south, and sit at table in the kingdom of God." (Luke 13:22-29)

A similar idea is suggested in the conclusion to the Parable of the Wise and Foolish Maidens.

> "Then the kingdom of heaven shall be compared to ten maidens who took their lamps and went to meet the bridegroom. Five of them were foolish and five were wise. For when the foolish took their lamps, they took no oil with them; but the wise took flasks of oil with their lamps. As the bridegroom was delayed, they all slumbered and slept. But at midnight there was a cry, 'Behold, the bridegroom! Come out to meet him.' Then all those maidens rose and trimmed their lamps. And the foolish said to the wise, 'Give us some of your oil, for our lamps are going out.' But the wise replied, 'Perhaps there will not be enough for us and for you; go rather to the dealers and buy for yourselves.' And while they went to buy, the bridegroom came, and those who were ready went in with him to the marriage feast; and the door was shut. Afterward the other maidens came also, saying, 'Lord, Lord, open to us.' But he replied, 'Truly, I say to you, I do not know you.' "[39]
>
> (Matthew 25:1-12 ‖ Mark 2:19-20)

The conception of the Kingdom having a door is in the background of Matthew 16:19, which states that the Kingdom's keys will be entrusted to Peter. For Jesus the Kingdom was like a city or fortress with gates that will be locked, opened, and closed.

---

[39]In the parallel Mark 2:19-20 Jesus explicitly refers to himself as the "bridegroom."

6. The Kingdom as the Antithesis of a Place of Torment

Repeatedly in Jesus' teachings the Kingdom is juxtaposed to a place of torment. Jesus' contemporaries faced the alternatives of enjoying bliss in the Kingdom or of enduring agony (frequently described as "weeping and gnashing of teeth") in a place of torment. Thus Mark 9:47-48 juxtaposes the Kingdom of God and hell.

> If your eye causes you to sin, pluck it out; it is better for you to enter the kingdom of god with one eye than with two eyes to be thrown into hell where their worm does not die, and the fire is not quenched.

Jesus' dual-destiny belief is reflected in the Matthean interpretations (Matthew 13:36-43, 47-50) given to the Parables of the Weeds and the Fishnet (both explicit Kingdom parables):

> His disciples came to him saying, "Explain to us the parable of the weeds of the field." He answered, "He who sows the good seed is the Son of Man; the field is the world, and the good seed means the sons of the kingdom, the weeds are the sons of the evil one, and the enemy who sowed them is the devil; the harvest is the close of the age, and the reapers are angels. Just as the weeds are gathered and burned with fire, so will it be at the close of the age. The Son of Man will send his angels, and they will gather out of his kingdom all causes of sin and all evil doers, and throw them into the furnace of fire; there men will weep and gnash their teeth. Then the righteous will shine like the sun in the kingdom of their Father." (Matthew 13:36b-43a)

> "Again, the kingdom of heaven is like a net which was thrown into the sea and gathered fish of every kind; when it was full, men drew it ashore and sat down and sorted the good into vessels but threw away the bad. So it will be at the close of the age. The angels will come out and separate the evil from the righteous, and throw them into the furnace of fire; there men will weep and gnash their teeth." (Matthew 13:47-50)

The weeping and gnashing of teeth detail crops up in Jesus' instruction about the narrow door (Luke 13:2-28). It appears in Jesus' laudatory comment about the centurion (Matthew 8:10-13), a comment that juxtaposes the Kingdom with "outer darkness":

> "Truly, I say to you, not even in Israel have I found such faith. I tell you, many will come from east and west and sit at table with Abraham, Isaac,

and Jacob in the kingdom of heaven, while the sons of the kingdom will be thrown into the outer darkness; there men will weep and gnash their teeth." (Matthew 8:10b-12)

7. The Kingdom's Arrival as Near in Time

For Jesus the Kingdom was not a remote goal of history—a dream to be realized hundreds or thousands of years in the future. Instead, the Kingdom was an impending wonder. The most forceful of Jesus' sayings emphasizing the Kingdom's nearness in time is his assertion preserved in Matthew 16:28 (paralleled in Mark 9:1 and Luke 9:27): "And he said to them, 'Truly, I say to you, there are some standing here who will not taste death before they see the Kingdom of God come with power.' " Or consider the Matthean summary of Jesus' message (Matthew 4:17). "From that time Jesus began to preach, saying, 'Repent, for the Kingdom of Heaven is at hand.' " Or note the instructions Jesus gave his disciples before sending them out on their preaching mission (Matthew 10:5-8): "These twelve Jesus sent out with the following instructions: 'Do not take the road to Gentile lands, and do not enter any Samaritan town; but go rather to the lost sheep of the house of Israel. And as you go proclaim the message: The Kingdom of Heaven is at hand.' " Jesus told his disciples during the Last Supper that it was the last Passover he would celebrate with them before the Kingdom came. This implies that he expected the Kingdom's arrival before the next Passover, when he would again drink wine with them (Luke 22:15-18, Matthew 26:29).

Thus—by way of summary—Jesus' Kingdom teachings involved the following factors:

1. Jesus expected a reconstitution of the tribes of Israel. He told his twelve disciples they would sit on thrones and judge the reconstituted tribes. They would also have the honor of sitting at Jesus' banquet table.
2. Jesus conceived of himself as God's future viceroy in the Kingdom of Heaven. On each side of his throne will be places of honor reserved for those for whom they have been prepared.
3. Entry in the Kingdom will be through a narrow door. Jesus will be the doorkeeper and the door keys will be entrusted to Peter.
4. Jesus anticipated the resurrection of Abraham, Isaac, Jacob, and the prophets. All will reappear and enjoy a good life in the Kingdom, participating in a messianic banquet in which many from east and west will also participate.

5. Apostate Jews will be expelled from the Kingdom. Those expelled will (from a place of torment outside) look into the Kingdom and behold the joys of those eating with Abraham, Isaac, and Jacob. Reflecting upon their unfortunate lot, they will weep and gnash their teeth. In contrast to this woeful existence, the righteous will shine like the sun in the Kingdom of their Father (Matthew 13:43).
6. Passover will be observed in the Kingdom. This observance will involve eating bread and drinking wine.
7. Physical necessities (food and clothing) will be provided. Those excluded from the Kingdom, however, will live in hunger (Luke 6:25).
8. In the Kingdom will be children, eunuchs, scribes, tax collectors, harlots, and the poor.
9. Within the Kingdom will be varying stations of honor. Some persons will be called great. Others will be called least.
10. The entry logia reveal that the Kingdom will be a territory that can be bodily entered. It will also be a place that can be seen with the eye.
11. Jesus expected the Kingdom to arrive in the near future—within the lifetime of his listeners. He sent out messengers to announce to Jews (but not to Gentiles) the Kingdom's near arrival.

The cumulative force of this evidence is obvious. Speaking in spatial categories, Jesus proclaimed the Kingdom's imminent coming for repentant Jews. The Synoptics portray Jesus as a prophet who drove himself relentlessly while proclaiming the good news of the Kingdom and who appointed apostles to go to all the villages and cities in Israel to announce that the Kingdom was near (Luke 9:2, Matthew 10:5-8).

At this point in our discussion, I invite your attention to "Appendix I" in which *every* verse in the Synoptics employing the word Kingdom (*basileia*) is quoted in full where you may peruse this evidence *for yourself*. I believe a perusal of the data found in "Appendix I" will reveal that the majority of Jesus' Kingdom statements correlate with the view that Jesus thought of the Kingdom as a blessed realm ("a heavenly city") that was soon to appear. This dual emphasis is found likewise in patristic literature, a relevant body of material that unfortunately is ignored by most New Testament exegetes. Thus, I invite your attention to "Appendix II" wherein is cited patristic evidence that—like the synoptic data—portrays the Kingdom as a place and as a future hope. This view was shared by thinkers like Clement, Polycarp, Irenaeus, and Tertullian, and dominated Christian thought until the time of Augustine, who identified the Kingdom with the Church, a view that still prevails in Roman Catholicism and in grassroots Protestantism.

III. A Hermeneutical Question

Having surveyed what Jesus taught concerning the Kingdom, we now confront an interpretive question: What hermeneutical theory best explains Jesus' observations concerning this Kingdom that was a blessed realm soon to appear? How should his words be interpreted? Should they be viewed figuratively or literally?[40] Should Jesus' words be taken at face value or should they be given symbolic signification?[41] At the present time (particularly in European theological circles and in American departments of religion associated with secular universities) the tendency prevails to give Jesus' words an at-face-value interpretation. This tendency is due to the recovery and systematic study of Jewish apocalyptic literature written immediately before and after the beginning of the Christian era. New Testament scholars and historians of religious thought are now aware that first-

---

[40]An aversion for interpreting literally the evidence that presents the kingdom as a spatial phenomenon can be seen in the following: Henri Clavier, "The Kingdom of God: Its Coming and Man's Entry in It," *Expository Times* 60 (June 1949): 241-44; S. Ivor Buse, "Spatial Imagery in New Testament Teaching about the Kingdom of God," *Expository Times* 60 (December 1948): 82; J. Grange Radford, "The Kingdom of God," *Expository Times* 46 (June 1935): 428-48; A. E. J. Rawlinson, "The Kingdom of God in the Apostolic Age," *Theology* 14 (May 1927): 262-66.

[41]An excellent example of symbolic interpretation of Jesus' language can be found in the turn-of-the-century *The Eschatology of the Gospels* by Ernst Von Dobschütz (London: Hodder and Stoughton, 1910). Writing concerning the messianic meal, he observed that
> As a matter of fact we find Jesus using the very words of being at table, eating bread and drinking the fruit of the vine in the kingdom of God (Matt. viii. 11; Luke xiii. 29, xiv. 15; Mark xiv. 25 c. par.); but here realistic interpretation is out of place; it is the popular way of expressing supreme happiness, which Jesus is using for something which is far beyond the literal sense of the words. Nobody I trust would imagine Jesus foretelling to his disciples the pleasures of a dinner in the Messianic kingdom, even when he takes the most realistic view of Jesus' eschatology. (119-20)

Or consider the remark by Langdon Gilkey in his *Message and Existence: An Introduction to Christian Theology* (New York: Winston-Seabury, 1979):
> By the Kingdom of God, or the reign of God, Jesus referred not to a place—surely not to a place above—but to the concrete ruling of God in the world, the actual or fulfilled sovereignty of God's will and purposes, and thus of the divine power among God's creatures. (165-66)

century Judaism was partially dominated by a conviction that the historical process was nearing its denouement. In epitome there was a belief that a coming Blessed Time, a Golden Age, was imminent for the Jewish people. A perusal of the writings of Alfred Loisy, Charles Guignebert, Millar Burrows, F. C. Grant, Maurice Goguel, Amos Wilder, Gustaf Dalman, Martin Dibelius, George Foot Moore, Rudolf Bultmann, Joachim Jeremias, Morton Scott Enslin, Albert Schweitzer, R. M. Grant, Martin Werner, Richard Hiers, and George Wesley Buchanan[42] will reveal that these exegetes believe the theory that accords best with New Testament evidence is the hypothesis that "Kingdom of God" was Jesus' distinctive way of referring to this Golden Age for which first-century Jews were expectantly waiting. These scholars contend that Jesus' language about a spatial Kingdom should be taken in a nonsubjective sense. Thus George Wesley Buchanan defined the Kingdom as a religious monarchy ''designed to exist on the same land as the Davidic Kingdom with its capital city at Jerusalem.''[43] This conception of the Kingdom as a theocratic territory was expressed years ago by Johannes Weiss as follows:

---

[42]Alfred Loisy, *The Origins of the New Testament,* trans. L. P. Jacks (New York: Macmillan, 1950) 33-55; Charles Guignebert, *Jesus,* trans. S. H. Hooke (New York, 1956) 325-52; Millar Burrows, "Thy Kingdom Come," *Journal of Biblical Literature* 74 (March 1955): 1-8; Frederick C. Grant, *The Gospel of the Kingdom* (New York: Macmillan, 1940) 131-32; Maurice Goguel, *The Life of Jesus,* trans. Olive Wyon (London: George Allen and Unwin Ltd., 1953) 562-86; Amos N. Wilder, *Eschatology and Ethics in the Teaching of Jesus* (New York: Harper and Brothers, 1950) 21-52; Gustaf Dalman, *The Words of Jesus,* trans. D. M. Kay (Edinburgh: T. & T. Clark, 1902) 91-139; Martin Dibelius, *Jesus,* trans. Charles Hedrick and Frederick C. Grant (Philadelphia: Fortress Press, 1939) 64-88; George Foot Moore, *Judaism* (Cambridge: Harvard University Press, 1954) 2:279-395 (an invaluable discussion of first-century Jewish beliefs concerning the imminence of a Golden Age); Rudolf Bultmann, *Theology of the New Testament,* vol. 1, trans. Kendrick Grobel (London: SCM Press, 1952; New York: Charles Scribners, 1951) 4-11; Joachim Jeremias, *Jesus' Promise to the Nations,* trans. S. H. Hooke (Naperville: Alec R. Allenson, 1958) 55-73; "Flesh and Blood Cannot Inherit the Kingdom of God," *New Testament Studies* 2 (January 1956): 151-59; Morton Scott Enslin, *Christian Beginnings* (New York: Harper & Brothers, 1938) 158-59; Albert Schweitzer, *The Mystery of the Kingdom of God,* trans. Walter Lowrie (New York: Macmillan Company, 1950); *The Quest of the Historical Jesus,* trans. W. Montgomery (London: Adam and Charles Black, 1954; New York: Macmillan, 1961); Robert M. Grant, "The Coming of the Kingdom," *Journal of Biblical Literature* 67 (September 1948): 297-303; Martin Werner, *The Formation of Christian Dogma,* trans. S. G. F. Brandon (London: Adams and Charles Black, 1957); Richard Hiers, *Jesus and the Future* (Atlanta: John Knox, 1981). George Wesley Buchanan: *Jesus: The King and His Kingdom* (Macon GA: Mercer University Press, 1984).

[43]Buchanan, *Jesus,* 191.

> The Kingdom of God as Jesus thought of it is never something subjective, inward, or spiritual, but is always the objective messianic Kingdom, which usually is pictured as a territory into which one enters, or as a land in which one has a share, or as a treasure which comes down from heaven.[44]

Moreover, the scholars cited above believe that Jesus expected the imminent arrival of this Golden Age. For him the Kingdom was not a remote goal of human history; rather, it was an impending miracle. This Kingdom's arrival, we can infer, would ipso facto abolish Roman control over Palestine. Consequently, in Roman eyes Jesus appeared to be an insurrectionist, and all four Gospels agree that Jesus was crucified by Pontius Pilate on the charge of being a Jewish pretender to the throne.

The strength of this Weissian-apocalyptic-eschatological understanding of the Kingdom is that it correlates (or harmonizes) with Jesus' recorded Kingdom sayings. This interpretation enables us to make sense of Jesus' Kingdom pronouncements. Yet Christian apologists do not relish this interpretation. Such is the case because an apocalyptic-eschatological view of the Kingdom opens a Pandora's box of problems.

One of these problems is *theological* in nature. Theology involves systematic reflection upon the Church's teachings, and across the centuries Christian spokesmen have assumed: "What Jesus taught is what the Church teaches. A continuity exists between Jesus' proclamation and the Church's proclamation." Capitulating to this longing for continuity, desiring to contemporize Jesus, Christians understandably want to believe that Jesus' Kingdom teachings are a vital part of the Christian faith. They have gladly accepted Augustine's view that the Kingdom is the Church, or Adolf von Harnack's view that the Kingdom is God's rule in men's hearts, or Walter Rauschenbusch's view that the Kingdom is the exercise of the moral life in society. But these views, enticing as they are, are impossible to reconcile with Jesus' recorded sayings about the Kingdom—sayings having to do with a reconstitution of the twelve tribes, with Passover observance, and with eating bread and drinking wine while sitting at banquet tables with Abraham, Isaac, and Jacob. Jesus' recorded sayings bring into focus the "strangeness," the "Jewishness," the "ideological remoteness" of Je-

---

[44]Johannes Weiss, *Jesus' Proclamation of the Kingdom of God*, trans. Richard Hiers and David Holland (Philadelphia: Fortress Press, 1971) 133.

sus' Kingdom beliefs. A remark of Julius Kaftan (quoted by Rudolf Bultmann) is unwelcome to theologians: "If the Kingdom of God is an eschatological matter, then it is a useless concept so far as dogmatics is concerned."[45]

Another problem broached by the Weissian-eschatological interpretation of the Kingdom is *Christological* in nature. We—as Christians—want to believe Jesus was infallible. We reason: "Jesus was the Son of God and thus spoke the truth and nothing but the truth." Yet devotees of the Weissian-eschatological view suggest Jesus was a mistaken prophet. Jesus expected the Kingdom's swift arrival, but this expected Kingdom did not appear. The Church, filled with Gentiles, appeared instead. I encountered this conception of Jesus as a mistaken prophet for the first time when I was a graduate student in seminary. This understanding of Jesus as a mistaken prophet troubled me then (in the 1950s); it troubles me now. I cringe when I read the following words written by Michael Grant, a secular historian:

> Jesus not only believed that God had ordered him to launch his Kingdom on earth, but he also maintained that this process would be completed very soon indeed: that the Day of the Lord was imminent, when God's will would reign everywhere, and the world, in some never wholly defined transcendent fashion would become perfect. This proved entirely wrong. The fulfillment did not take place, and has still not taken place. So, the whole ministry of Jesus was founded on a mistake.[46]

I also cringe when I read these sentences by Hans Küng, the Tübingen theologian:

> The question then becomes so much more urgent: is not this proclamation of the Kingdom of God in the last resort simply a form of late Jewish apocalyptic? Is not Jesus ultimately an apocalyptic fanatic? Was he not under an illusion? In a word, was he not mistaken? Strictly speaking, we need not have any dogmatic inhibitions about admitting this in certain circumstances. To err is human. And if Jesus of Nazareth was truly man,

---

[45]Ibid., 24. This Bultmann note appears in the introduction by Richard Hiers and David Holland to the English translation of Weiss's *Die Predigt Jesus vom Reiche Gottes*.

[46]Michael Grant, *Jesus: An Historian's Review of the Gospels* (New York: Charles Scribner's Sons, 1973) 193-94.

he could also err. Of course there are some theologians who are more afraid of error in this connection than they are of sin, death, and the devil.[47]

This final observation by Professor Küng reflects still another problem raised by a Weissian-eschatological interpretation of the Kingdom—*a professional problem*. Frequently overlooked is the institutional context within which theologians and New Testament scholars work. Many teach in denominational colleges or in seminaries where the mere questioning of Jesus' infallibility would be professional suicide. On ecclesiastical payrolls, they are expected to make Jesus' teachings meaningful and relevant. Thus, to believe Jesus was in error about his major message—the Kingdom of God—is for them a closed option. This explains, I believe, why many New Testament exegetes have been attracted to C. H. Dodd's hypothesis of realized eschatology. Dodd's hypothesis is a "scholarly" trapdoor through which they can escape from the hermeneutical house constructed by Johannes Weiss and Albert Schweitzer.

If intellectual integrity is to be maintained, however, we—as Christians—ought to respect the dictum: honest exegesis and careful historical research must not be influenced (or intimidated) by possibly adverse theological repercussions caused by exegesis and historical research. The evidence should be followed where it leads. Christian thinkers do not "serve God" through intellectual dishonesty or through evidence gerrymandering (and evidence can be slanted merely by including and excluding information).

Having expressed these caveats, I conclude this chapter by observing that scholars such as Johannes Weiss, Albert Schweitzer, and Martin Dibelius were correct: Jesus' Kingdom preaching was predicated on a mistake. His fervent belief that the Kingdom would appear on earth within his listeners' lifetime was an error, an illusion, an unfulfilled hope. To me this conclusion is as unwelcome as it is unsought. In this book's last chapter, I shall return to this unwelcome conclusion and explore its implications for Christian theology and preaching.

---

[47]Hans Küng, *On Being a Christian* (New York: Doubleday, 1976) 271-81.

CHAPTER
• 4 •

The Kingdom Version of Realized Eschatology

In this book's preface, I observed that two versions of realized eschatology appear in Professor Dodd's writings: a *Kingdom version* and a *Christological version*. I will discuss the *Christological version* of realized eschatology in the next chapter. This chapter will be devoted to the *Kingdom version*. By the *Kingdom version* I refer to Professor Dodd's contention that the Kingdom of God was present—or was realized—in Jesus' ministry. This version, I will argue, is untenable. It is a hermeneutical castle built upon exegetical quicksand.

Professor Dodd developed what I am calling a *Kingdom version* of realized eschatology in his 1935 book *The Parables of the Kingdom*. He based his thesis that the Kingdom of God was actualized in Jesus' ministry upon the following synoptic passages:

1. *The Casting Out of Demons Logion* (Matthew 12:28 ‖ Luke 11:20)
   But if it is by the finger of God [Mt; the Spirit of God, Lk] that I cast out the demons, then the Kingdom of God has come upon you.

2. *The Message to John the Baptist* (Matthew 11:4-6 ‖ Luke 7:22-23)
   Go and tell John what you hear and see: the blind receive their sight and the lame walk, lepers are cleansed and the deaf hear, and the dead are raised up, and the poor have good news preached to them. And blessed is he who takes no offense at me.

3. *The Markan Gospel Summary* (Mark 1:14-15)
   Now after John was arrested, Jesus came into Galilee, preaching the gospel of God, and saying, "The time is fulfilled, and the Kingdom of God is at hand; repent, and believe the gospel."

4. *The Beatitude of Hearing and Seeing* (Matthew 13:16-17 || Luke 10:23-24)

   Blessed are the eyes that see what you see; for I tell you that many prophets and Kings wished to see what you see, and did not see it, and to hear what you hear and did not hear it.

5. *The Men of Nineveh and Queen of the South Condemnation* (Matthew 12:41-42 || Luke 11:32, 31)

   The men of Nineveh will arise at the judgment with this generation and condemn it; for they repented at the preaching of Jonah, and behold, something greater than Jonah is here. The Queen of the South will arise at the judgment with this generation and condemn it; for she came from the ends of the earth to hear the wisdom of Solomon, and behold, something greater than Solomon is here.

6. *The Violence Remark* (Matthew 11:12-13; cf. Luke 16:16)

   From the days of John the Baptist until now the Kingdom of heaven has suffered violence, and men of violence take it by force. For all the prophets and the law prophesied until John.

With reference to these six statements Professor Dodd stated that

> these passages, the most explicit of their kind, are sufficient to show that in the earliest tradition Jesus was understood to have proclaimed that the Kingdom of God, the hope of many generations, had at last come.[1]

An examination of these six passages, however, will reveal that this confident statement by Professor Dodd is not justified. *Three of them* (the John the Baptist Message in Matthew 11:4-6, the Beatitude of Hearing and Seeing in Matthew 13:16-17, and the Men of Nineveh and Queen of the South Condemnation in Matthew 12:41-42) *do not contain the phrase "Kingdom of God."* To construct an interpretation of the Kingdom on statements that do not contain the term is a curious and unsound hermeneutical procedure. Moreover, Professor Dodd subsequently referred to another of the passages (the Violence Remark of Matthew 11:12-13 || Luke 16:16) as a "notorious *crux interpretum*" and observed, "I am not at all sure that I understand it."[2] His interpretation of a fifth passage (Mark 1:14-15) involved mistaken Septuagint evidence.

---

[1] C. H. Dodd, *The Parables of the Kingdom* (London: James Nisbet and Company, 1935) 48-49.

[2] Ibid., v.

The crucial passage for Professor Dodd, as I observed previously, is Matthew 12:28 || Luke 11:20, which asserts, "If I by the Spirit of God [Lk: finger of God] cast out the demons, then the Kingdom of God has come upon you." I agree with Millar Burrows's observation that when all the evidence in the sayings of Jesus for realized eschatology has been thoroughly tested, it boils down to this Jesus logion of Matthew 12:28 || Luke 11:20.[3] Indeed, the edifice of realized eschatology (that is, the Kingdom version) is constructed on the sole foundation stone of Matthew 12:28 || Luke 11:20, and as I observed in the preface, this statement ("If I by the Spirit of God cast out the demons, then the Kingdom of God has come upon you") has become for numerous exegetes *the hermeneutical cornerstone* for understanding what Jesus meant by the Kingdom of God. Professor Dodd found in this statement "evidence" that the *Kingdom* was a curative *reign* or *power* operative in Jesus' exorcisms. He was able to advance this interpretation because the Greek word for *Kingdom* (*basileia*) can mean either "reign" ("rule") or "Kingdom" in the sense of a territory ruled by a king. Whether *basileia* means "reign" or "Kingdom" depends upon its use in a given context. Time and again in *The Parables of the Kingdom* Professor Dodd assigned to *basileia* the abstract meaning of "reign" or "power"; this "reign" was manifest as a curative power in Jesus' exorcisms. Jesus' exorcisms, so Professor Dodd reasoned, were evidence of the Kingdom's actual arrival.

This line of reasoning, I believe, is fallacious. To understand this fallacy, however, it will be necessary to examine the Synoptists' understanding of Jesus' healing-exorcistic miracles. Thus this chapter begins with a necessary excursus on Jesus' healing ministry. Only after an understanding has been reached on *how the Synoptists viewed Jesus' healing-exorcistic activities* will it be possible for us to deal critically with Dodd's interpretation of these same activities. The relevance of the following digression to the overall discussion will become obvious in the second part of this chapter.

I. An Excursus on Jesus' Healing Ministry

Vernon McCasland once observed that "to determine how Jesus regarded himself is the most difficult problem of New Testament scholar-

---

[3]Millar Burrows, "Thy Kingdom Come," *Journal of Biblical Literature* 74 (March 1955): 5.

ship."[4] This vexing problem exists because the data is complex. It exists also because of the difficulty of distinguishing between data representing Jesus' thought and data reflecting the early Church's theology. Nevertheless, let us focus attention upon three words that are parts of these Christological data explaining Jesus. The three are *dunamis, exousia,* and *pneuma. Dunamis* (δύναμις)—from which we get such English words as *dynamic* and *dynamite*—is usually translated as *power; exousia* (ἐξουσία) as *authority*; and *pneuma* (πηεῦμα) as *spirit*. These three words are employed repeatedly in the Synoptics in connection with Jesus' healing-exorcistic ministry. They are technical terms used to designate the divine power or energy that made possible Jesus' healings and exorcisms. Let us give attention to their use in the Synoptics.

The view that Jesus was endowed with *dunamis* is expressed vividly in the pericope about the woman with a flow of blood (Mark 5:25-34). This Markan account reads in part as follows.

> She had heard the reports about Jesus, and came up behind him in the crowd and touched his garment. For she said, "If I touch even his garments, I shall be made well." And immediately the hemorrhage ceased; and she felt in her body that she was healed of her disease. And Jesus, perceiving in himself that power [δύναμις] had gone forth from him, immediately turned about in the crowd, and said, "Who touched my garments?" (Mark 5:27-30)

This statement suggests that Jesus was aware of an indwelling *dunamis* that enabled him to heal. As Rudolf Bultmann pointed out, this curative power emanating from Jesus functioned automatically.[5] Over and over again in the Synoptics the idea is expressed that by coming into physical contact with Jesus one availed oneself of Jesus' healing power.[6] By metonymy αἱ δυνάμεις is used to designate the "mighty [healing] works" of Jesus (for example, Mark 6:2), and in Acts 2:22 Peter declared that the δυνάμεις

---

[4]Vernon McCasland, *By the Finger of God* (New York: Macmillan, 1951) 10.

[5]Rudolf Bultmann, *History of the Synoptic Tradition,* trans. John Marsh (London: Basil Blackwell; New York: Harper & Row, 1963) 219.

[6]Over and over in the Synoptics the idea is expressed that by coming into physical contact with Jesus one availed himself of Jesus' healing power. Note the following: Matthew 8:3; 9:18, 29; 14:36; 20:34; Mark 1:31, 41; 3:5, 10; 5:23, 27, 41; 6:2, 5, 56; 7:32, 33; 8:22, 25; 10:13; Luke 4:40; 5:13; 6:19; 8:46, 54; 11:13; 22:51.

of Jesus were done by God. In Mark 6:14 there is ascribed to Herod a recognition that "powers" (δυνάμεις) were at work in Jesus.

The *dunamis* idea is expressed in the Third Gospel in this manner:

> And he came down with them and stood on a level place, with a great crowd of his disciples and a great multitude of people from all Judea and Jerusalem and the seacoast of Tyre and Sidon, who came to hear him and to be healed of their diseases; and those who were troubled with unclean spirits were cured. And all the crowd sought to touch him, for power [δύναμις] came forth from him and healed them all. (Luke 6:17-19)

> On one of those days, as he was teaching, there were Pharisees and teachers of the law sitting by, who had come from every village of Galilee and Judea and from Jerusalem; and the power [δύναμις] of the Lord was with him to heal. (Luke 5:17)

The meaning of such sayings is clear: Jesus could perform healings because he was endowed with a curative *dunamis*. The belief that the *dunamis* of God was active in Jesus is found repeatedly in the Pauline epistles. In 1 Corinthians 1:24 Jesus is called the "power of God"; in 1 Corinthians 6:14 and 2 Corinthians 13:4 the idea is expressed that the "power of God" raised Jesus from the dead.

Closely related to this *dunamis* concept is the idea of Jesus being endued with *exousia*. That *dunamis* and *exousia* are similar concepts is obvious from their collocation in Luke 4:36, a verse that appears in the record of a demon exorcism at Capernaum.

> And in the synagogue there was a man who had the spirit of an unclean demon; and he cried out with a loud voice, "Ah! What have you to do with us, Jesus of Nazareth? Have you come to destroy us? I know who you are, the Holy One of God." But Jesus rebuked him, saying, "Be silent, and come out of him!" And when the demon had thrown him down in the midst, he came out of him, having done him no harm. And they were all amazed and said to one another, "What is this word? For with authority [ἐξουσία] and power [δύναμις] he commands the unclean spirits, and they come out."[7] (Luke 4:33-36)

---

[7] It cannot be argued that *exousia* was used only with reference to Jesus' teaching, while *dunamis* was used with reference to Jesus' healing ministry. In Luke 4:32 there is the observation that the teaching of Jesus was with *exousia;* but only four verses later (Luke 4:36) there is the statement that with *exousia* Jesus cast out the unclean spirits.

70 • Rethinking Realized Eschatology

In Mark 11:27-33 inquiry is made of Jesus as to the nature of the *exousia* by which he did his mighty works. The answer ("And Jesus said to them, 'Neither will I tell you by what *exousia* I do these things.' ") implies Jesus was aware of a preternatural *exousia* that enabled him to perform healing deeds, but to the hostile and unbelieving he refused to reveal its nature.[8]

Moreover, the Gospels portray Jesus as endowing his disciples with *exousia* that enabled them to heal the sick and cast out unclean spirits.

> And he called to him his twelve disciples and gave them authority [ἐξουσία] over unclean spirits, to cast them out, and to heal every disease and every infirmity.[9] (Matthew 10:1)

> And he called to him the twelve, and began to send them out two by two, and gave them authority [ἐξουσία] over the unclean spirits. . . . And so they went out and preached that men should repent. And they cast out many demons, and annointed with oil many that were sick and healed them. (Mark 6:7; 12:13)

The Synoptics ascribe Jesus' pedagogic abilities to the indwelling *exousia*. Thus Matthew asserts,

> And when Jesus finished these sayings, the crowds were astonished at this teaching, for he taught them as one who had authority [ἐξουσία], and not as their scribes.[10] (Matthew 7:28-29)

Likewise, the Gospels depict Jesus as having *exousia* to forgive sins. In recounting the healing of a paralytic these words appear:

> And behold, they brought to him a paralytic, lying on his bed; and when Jesus saw their faith he said to the paralytic, "Take heart, my son; your sins are forgiven." And behold, some of the scribes said to themselves, "This man is blaspheming." But Jesus, knowing their thoughts, said, "Why do you think evil in your hearts? For which is easier, to say, 'Your sins are forgiven,' or to say 'Rise and walk'? But that you may know that the Son of man has authority [ἐξουσία] on earth to forgive sins"—he

---

[8]Note that in Acts 4:7 an inquiry is made of the apostles similar to the inquiry made of Jesus in Mark 11:27-33.

[9]The same idea is expressed in Mark 3:15; Luke 9:1; and Luke 10:19.

[10]Cf. Luke 4:32 and Mark 1:22.

then said to the paralytic—"Rise, take up your bed and go home." When the crowds saw it, they were afraid, and they glorified God, who had given such authority [ἐξουσία] to men. (Matthew 9:2-8)

The meaning of these sayings is obvious: because Jesus was endued with *exousia* he surpassed the scribes in pedagogic ability, cast out demons, and forgave sins.[11]

Related to endowment with preternatural *dunamis* and *exousia* is Jesus' endowment with the *pneuma* of God—an endowment the Synoptics portray as taking place at the baptism. Many exegetes, familiar with theology's Trinitarian dogma, overlook the early Church's unsophisticated conception of *pneuma* possession. Based upon an animistic view, *pneuma* possession is parallel in meaning to Jesus' endowment with *dunamis* and *exousia*.

In the Synoptics Jesus was accused by opponents of exorcising demons by Beelzebub's power. In both Matthew and Mark the retort to this Beelzebub slur is the unforgivable sin statement that appears in Mark as follows:

Truly, I say to you, all sins will be forgiven the sons of men, and whatever blasphemies they utter; but whoever blasphemes against the Holy Spirit never has forgiveness, but is guilty of an eternal sin—for they had said, "He has an unclean spirit." (Mark 3:28-30)

The retort's implied teaching is that by the Spirit of God (rather than by Beelzebub) Jesus exorcised demonic spirits. This teaching is explicitly expressed in Matthew 12:28, "But if it is by the Spirit of God that I cast out the demons. . . . " Thus the New Testament not only portrays Jesus as exorcising demons by *dunamis* and *exousia,* but also by the *pneuma* of God.

The conception of the Holy Spirit as an instrument of God's activity (and the similarity in meaning between *pneuma* and *dunamis*) appears in the Lukan account of Jesus' miraculous birth. In Luke's Infancy Narrative there is a paralleling of *pneuma* and *dunamis* as follows:

The Holy Spirit [πνεῦμα] will come upon you
And the power [δύναμις] of the Most High will overshadow you;
Therefore the child to be born will be called holy,
The Son of God. (Luke 1:35)

---

[11]Note that in Luke 12:5 God is described as having *exousia* to cast into hell.

Or consider the summary statement in Luke 4:14 that asserts,

> And Jesus returned in the power of the Spirit [δύναμει τοῦ πνεύματος] into Galilee, and a report concerning him went out through all the surrounding country. (Luke 4:14)

The affinity in meaning between *dunamis* and *pneuma* can also be observed in the command of Luke 24:49 and the fulfillment of this command at the Pentecost festival. The disciples were commanded by the Risen Lord not to leave Jerusalem until they were clothed with *dunamis* from on high; this clothing with *dunamis* took place with the descent of the *pneuma* on the disciples during the Pentecost season. Thus, in Acts 1:8 there is the statement, "But you shall receive power [*dunamis*] when the Holy Spirit has come upon you."

The juxtaposition of *pneuma* and *dunamis* also appears in the primitive Christological hymn of Acts 10, which declares in part,

> You know the word which he sent to Israel, preaching good news of peace by Jesus Christ (he is Lord of all), the word which was proclaimed throughout all Judea, beginning from Galilee after the baptism which John preached: how God anointed Jesus of Nazareth *with the Holy Spirit and with Power;* how he went about doing good and healing all that were oppressed by the devil, for God was with him. (Acts 10:36-38)

To reach an understanding of these ascriptions to Jesus of preternatural *dunamis, exousia,* and *pneuma* is no easy hermeneutical task. The most meaningful discussion of this issue that I have encountered is Alan Richardson's *The Miracle-Stories of the Gospels*. In his study, Richardson argued that *dunamis, exousia,* and *pneuma* are not to be understood metaphysically as hypostatized intermediate beings emanating from God (such a hypostatization would be contrary to Jewish monotheism).[12] Rather, the utilization of these terms represents a convenience or perhaps even a necessity of language.[13] They are synonyms that convey the *same general meaning*, and that general meaning is *God was in Christ*. In New Testament thought *dunamis, exousia,* and *pneuma* are agents or instruments of God's activity in Jesus and in his disciples. Because of his endowment with

---

[12] Alan Richardson, *The Miracle-Stories of the Gospels* (London: SCM Press, 1941) 6.
[13] Ibid.

dunamis, exousia, and *pneuma,* Jesus was empowered to perform miracles of healing and to cast out demonic spirits. It is difficult to cast off the mistaken idea that Jesus performed mighty works and exorcisms as proof of *his own* supernatural greatness. Jesus did not possess such a self-exalting attitude; for Jesus (and the early Church) his miracles were possible because God had given him power to perform them.

Thus the Synoptics speak of Jesus' curative deeds as acts of power (*dunameis*), signs (*semeia*), and works (*erga*), terms that reflect the biblical conception of God as power. Properly speaking, our word *miracle,* which conveys the sense of a *deus ex machina* in a closed system of natural law, is semantically and ideologically unsuitable to designate Jesus' curative acts.

Moreover, from the preceding study of New Testament evidence one *negative conclusion* must be noted: *nowhere in the New Testament* (unless one accepts Dodd's exegesis of Matthew 12:28) *is there a suggestion that Jesus or the early Church ascribed Jesus' healings and exorcisms to basileia.* Nowhere is there a statement that says in substance, "And the *basileia* of the Lord was with him to heal and to exorcise" (which would be a parallel to Luke 5:17). Jesus' healings and exorcisms are repeatedly ascribed in the New Testament to *dunamis, exousia,* and *pneuma, but not once to basileia.* This negative conclusion is significant because realized eschatologists insist on conceiving of *basileia* as a healing-exorcistic "reign" or "power," an insistence that is contrary to New Testament thought patterns.

The New Testament distinction between *basileia* on the one hand and *dunamis* and *exousia* on the other hand, is set forth in Luke 9:1-2:

> And he called the twelve together and gave them power [δύναμις] and authority [ἐξουσία] over all demons and to cure diseases, and he sent them out to preach the kingdom [βασιλεία] of God and to heal.

This quotation shows that for the Synoptists the Kingdom of God was the subject of proclamation (note Matthew 4:23; 9:35; 13:19; 24:14; Luke 4:43; 8:1; 9:1-2, 11b, 60; 16:16), while demons were expelled and diseases were cured because of the effective operation of God's *dunamis* and *exousia*. *To ascribe Jesus' exorcisms and healing miracles to the operation of a curative basileia is to confuse New Testament thought categories.* More consideration will be given to this confusing of categories in the discussion of Dodd's hermeneutics that follows.

74 • Rethinking Realized Eschatology

II. The Six Crucial Passages

Let us now focus our attention on the six crucial passages ("the most explicit of their kind") that Professor Dodd used as the biblical basis for his "Kingdom version" of realized eschatology. These passages, Professor Dodd asserted, "are sufficient to show that in the earliest tradition Jesus was understood to have proclaimed that the Kingdom of God, the hope of many generations, had at last come."[14] The tenuousness of this data, I believe, will become obvious.

1. The Casting Out of Demons Logion
(Matthew 12:28 || Luke 11:20)

An intriguing feature of the Synoptics is their candid disclosure of criticisms leveled against Jesus by his contemporaries. Because of Jesus' camaraderie with apostate Jews, for example, his enemies referred to him as a glutton, a drunkard, and a friend of tax collectors and sinners.[15] The logion of Matthew 12:28 || Luke 11:20 appears in a pericope that contains probably the most cutting insult leveled against Jesus. Witnessing his exorcistic activity, the Pharisees accused Jesus of being in league with Beelzebul, the "lord of manure."[16] Jesus responded to his calumniators by declaring,

> If I cast out demons by the dung god, by whom do your sons cast them out? But if it is by the Spirit of God [Mt; finger of God, Lk] that I cast out demons, then the kingdom of God has come upon you.
> (Matthew 12:28 || Luke 11:19-20)

In his exegesis of this logion, Dodd assumed that *basileia* had an *abstract* meaning of "reign" or "power" or "sovereignty." Moreover, Dodd argued that this abstract *basileia* was the agent of God's activity in Christ whereby demon exorcisms were accomplished. Thus with reference to *basileia* he wrote:

---

[14]Dodd, *The Parables of the Kingdom*, 48-49.

[15]E.g., Matthew 11:19 || Luke 7:34.

[16]While the true etymology and meaning are not certain, "Beelzebul" may be בַּעַל ("lord") plus the Talmudic זְבוּל ("dung"), akin to or a variant of the O.T. בַּעַל זְבוּב ("Beelzebub," "lord of flies," e.g., 2 Kings 1:2ff.).

Something has happened, which has not happened before, and which means that the sovereign power of God has come into effective operation. It is not a matter of having God for your King in the sense that you obey His commandments: it is a matter of being confronted with the power of God at work in the world. In other words, the "eschatological" Kingdom of God is proclaimed as a present fact, which men must recognize, whether by their actions they accept or reject it.[17]

In this statement Dodd *equated the Kingdom of God with the power of God in Christ*. That Dodd conceived of *basileia* (sovereignty) as the agent of God's activity in Christ is palpable from the following quotation from *The Parables of the Kingdom* wherein "Kingdom" is defined as "divine power."

> The common idea, as we have seen, underlying all uses of the term "The Kingdom of God" is that of the manifest and effective assertion of the divine sovereignty against all the evil of the world. . . . In the ministry of Jesus Himself the divine power is released in effective conflict with evil. "If I by the finger of God cast out demons, then the Kingdom of God has come upon you."[18]

There can be no doubt that the logion of Matthew 12:28 || Luke 11:20 is the proof text par excellence of realized eschatology.[19] Matthew 12:28 was, as Krister Stendahl observed in a lecture at the Harvard Divinity School, C. H. Dodd's "golden nugget." If an exegete accepts Dodd's abstract understanding of *basileia* as "divine power," and if Matthew 12:28 || Luke 11:20 is viewed as a synonymous parallelism and is interpreted in isolation from the rest of synoptic data dealing with exorcisms and the Kingdom of God, then one could argue on the basis of this logion that the *basileia* arrived with Jesus.

This line of reasoning has become common in Anglo-American biblical studies and is found, for example, in Marcus Borg's magnificent

---

[17]Dodd, *The Parables of the Kingdom*, 44 (1961 rev. ed., 29).

[18]Ibid., 50 (1961 rev. ed., 35). On page 76 Dodd writes, "Let us then go back to the common underlying meaning of the expression 'The Kingdom of God' in all its various uses. It means God's exercising his kingly rule among men. In particular it implies that the divine power is effectively at issue with the evil of the world."

[19]For an indication of how widely Dodd's exegesis of this verse has been accepted note G. E. P. Cox, *The Gospel According to St. Matthew* (Oxford: Clarendon Press, 1945) 190; N.B. Stonehouse, *The Witness of Luke to Christ* (London: Tyndale Press, 1951) 154.

Conflict, Holiness, and Politics in the Teachings of Jesus. Therein the Kingdom is defined as a "primordial beneficent power." Commenting upon Matthew 12:28 ‖ Luke 11:20 ("a saying universally accepted as authentic"), Professor Borg observed:

> A saying universally accepted as authentic and commonly regarded as a central key for understanding Jesus' use of the symbol connects the Kingdom of God to exorcism: "But if it is by the finger (or "Spirit") of God that I cast out demons, then the Kingdom of God has come upon you." Most discussions of this verse note that it is authentic, speaks of the Kingdom as present, and links the coming of the Kingdom to the casting out of demons and therefore to the defeat of Satan, the ruler of the present age, all of which is correct. Often overlooked, however, is a connection of signal importance: the passage joins Jesus' use of Kingdom of God to the religious experience of a holy man, for exorcism is a classic activity of a holy man.

Professor Borg continued:

> The explicit connection made by this verse between Jesus' exorcistic activity as a holy man and his use of the phrase Kingdom of God has an immediate implication. Kingdom of God here is Jesus' designation or "name" for the primordial beneficent power of the other realm, an energy which can become active in ordinary reality and which flows through him in his exorcisms. Expressed in language drawn from the religious history of Judaism, Jesus' exorcisms were the Kingdom of God manifested within the world of history; expressed in language drawn from the intellectual tradition of the history of religions, his exorcisms were the "power of the holy" entering the profane world. The same reality is designated by both expressions. In short, the phrase Kingdom of God does not refer to a concept or ideal or belief, but to an actual though not physical reality: the beneficent power of the other realm. In the exorcisms, that power "comes": "But if it is by the finger of God that I cast out demons, then the Kingdom of God has come upon you."[20]

Exegesis of a particular statement of scripture, however, is not something to be "done in a corner." In attempting to understand a Jesus logion, it is sound hermeneutical procedure to give attention to *all relevant syn-*

---

[20]Marcus Borg, *Conflict, Holiness, and Politics in the Teaching of Jesus* (New York: Edwin Mellen Press, 1984) 252-54.

optic data. I am convinced that when all synoptic evidence is brought to bear on Matthew 12:28 || Luke 11:20, Dodd's interpretation of this logion (adopted unreservedly by scholars such as Professor Borg) becomes untenable. Attention will now be given to the vulnerability of Dodd's exegesis of this logion.

a. The Confusing of Basileia with Pneuma

The variant in Matthew 12:28 || Luke 11:20 of "Spirit of God" and "finger of God" is well known. Jesus probably used the latter expression, and the former represents Matthew's avoidance of an anthropomorphism. Yet the meanings of these two expressions are identical: both denote the dynamic activity of God in Christ.

The first part of this chapter argued that in synoptic thought Jesus performed miracles and cast out demonic spirits because of his endowment with *dunamis, exousia,* and *pneuma* from God. Bearing in mind that in the Synoptics *pneuma* is the *agent of God's activity* in demon exorcism, I find it puzzling that Dodd in his exegesis of Matthew 12:28 || Luke 11:20 ignored the reference to *pneuma*. Dodd did not give attention to the phrase "If I by the *pneuma* of God cast out the demons. . . . " Instead, he focused his attention on the phrase "then the kingdom of God has come upon you." In other words, Dodd considered abstract *basileia* to be the instrument of God's activity in Christ. But his ignoring the reference to the Spirit is indefensible. In this logion it is not the "power of the Kingdom" that is at work. Nor is the "Kingdom of God" described as being operative. Rather the Spirit is operative. The point of the Beelzebul pericope (Matthew 12:22-32 || Luke 11:14-23) is that through the Spirit of God (not by the "lord of manure") Jesus cast out demons.[21] The emphasis in the Beelzebul pericope upon the Spirit as the instrument of God's activity in Christ is particularly plain in Matthew's gospel. This pericope is preceded by the citing (Matthew 12:18-21) of Isaiah 42:1-4, which reads in part,

---

[21]That the Spirit of God was the agent of the exorcisms of Jesus in Matthew 12:28 was readily recognized in patristic exegesis. Note the following citations from Augustine. *On the Holy Trinity* 11.22, as in Arthur West Haddan, *On the Holy Trinity. Doctrinal Treatises. Moral Treatises,* vol. 3 of *A Select Library of the Nicene and Post-Nicene Fathers of the Christian Church,* Philip Schaff, ed., 14 vols. (New York: Christian Literature Company, 1887) 30; *On the Blasphemy Against the Holy Ghost* 25, as in R. G. MacMullen, *Saint Augustine: Sermon on the Mount. Harmony of the Gospels. Homilies on the Gospels,* vol. 6 of ibid. (1888) 327.

> Behold, my servant whom I have chosen,
> My beloved with whom my soul is well pleased.
> I will put my spirit upon him,
> And he shall proclaim justice to the Gentiles. (Matthew 12:18)

Immediately following this pronouncement that Jesus was endowed with the spirit as predicted by Isaiah, Matthew placed the Beelzebul controversy, which climaxes in Jesus' retort to his critics that by the Spirit of God he cast out demons. Devotees of realized eschatology overlook the grammatical structure of this retort. The Greek text reads,

> εἰ δὲ ἐν πνεύματι θεοῦ ἐγὼ ἐκβάλλω τὰ δαιμόνια, ἄρα ἔφθασεν ἐφ' ὑμᾶς ἡ βασιλεία τοῦ θεοῦ.

Syntactically, this retort is a first-class conditional sentence (the condition is assumed to be true or fulfilled). Thus, the verse can be structurally analyzed:

> PROTASIS: If I by the spirit of God cast out the demons, (if clause)
> APODOSIS: then the Kingdom of God has come upon you. (conclusion)

The protasis presupposes—assumes as true—that the "spirit of God" (*not* the "power of the Kingdom") was the agency by which Jesus cast out demons. The apodosis expresses a conclusion that naturally follows, "then the Kingdom of God has come upon you." Yet Professor Dodd, ignoring the protasis, "found" the agency of demon exorcism in the apodosis, that is, in "Kingdom," defined by Professor Dodd as "sovereign power." About this "Kingdom" he wrote, "Something has happened which has not happened before, and which means that the sovereign power of God has come into effective operation. . . . It is a matter of being confronted with the power of God at work in the world."[22] But this conceiving of "Kingdom" (in the sense of "sovereign power") *as the exorcistic agency* does not agree syntactically with the protasis that designates "spirit of God" *as the exorcistic agency*.

Matthew's "spirit of God" emphasis explains why a solemn warning immediately follows.

> Therefore I tell you, every sin and blasphemy will be forgiven men, but the blasphemy against the Spirit will not be forgiven. And whoever says

---

[22]Dodd, *The Parables of the Kingdom*, 44.

> a word against the Son of man will be forgiven; but whoever speaks against the Holy Spirit will not be forgiven, either in this age or in the age to come. (Matthew 13:31-32)

Thus Matthew repeatedly emphasizes that *through the agency of the Holy Spirit Jesus ruled demonic powers*. Perhaps the best commentary on the verses just noted is the following extract from an early Christological hymn preserved in Acts.

> You know the word which he sent to Israel, preaching good news of peace by Jesus Christ . . . how God anointed Jesus of Nazareth *with the Holy Spirit and with power;* how he went about doing good and *healing all that were oppressed by the devil,* for God was with him.
> (Acts 10:36, 38)

Thus, Dodd missed the point of the Beelzebul pericope when he ascribed Jesus' exorcisms to *basileia* rather than to the spirit of God. The insight cannot be too strongly emphasized that nowhere in the New Testament (unless one accepts Dodd's esoteric interpretation of Matthew 12:28) is there any suggestion that *basileia* was considered the agent of God's activity in Christ. The Kingdom of God is an *object of prayer, the subject of a proclamation,* and *a future hope,* while the spirit of God (with *dunamis* and *exousia*) is the instrument of God's dynamic activity in Christ by which healings and exorcisms were accomplished.

b. The Frequency of Exorcism in the First Century

Devotees of realized eschatology overlook the frequency of demon exorcism in the first century. A reading of *By the Finger of God* by S. Vernon McCasland and *Possession, Demoniacal and Other* by T. K. Oesterreich reveals that among both Jews and Gentiles exorcism was a commonly accepted phenomenon. Indeed, Jews specialized in demon exorcism, and Jesus recognized the ability of fellow Jews to cast out unclean spirits.

Kenneth W. Clark recognized, however, that this frequency of demon exorcism raises a problem for the realized eschatologist.

> One is tempted to inquire why the reported activity of exorcism by Jesus at this time can be construed so uniquely to mean that the Kingdom of God is already and for the first time in "effective operation," while the

reports of similar activity by other exorcists at other times are found to yield no such conclusion.[23]

If demon exorcism signified that the Kingdom had come, could it be argued that the Kingdom also arrived when Tobias expelled a demon with smoke from the heart and liver of a fish?[24] In other words, if Jesus' exorcisms "meant" the Kingdom had arrived, why did not exorcisms by Jewish exorcists also "mean" the Kingdom had arrived? Rudolf Bultmann recognized this dilemma—a dilemma implied in Matthew 12:27-28, which affirms,

> And if I cast out demons by Beelzebul, by whom do your sons cast them out? Therefore they shall be your judges. But if it is by the spirit of God that I cast out demons, then the kingdom of God has come upon you.

But Bultmann believed Matthew 12:27 and Matthew 12:28 were originally unattached sayings. Otherwise, so Bultmann wrote, "if the connection between Matthew 12:27 and Matthew 12:28 were original, it would follow that the Jewish exorcists also cast out demons by the Spirit, and that their activity also demonstrated the coming of the Kingdom."[25] Dodd had no right to read into Jesus' exorcisms a unique significance, namely, that the Kingdom of God had come, while not ascribing the same significance to other first-century exorcisms.

c. A Hermeneutical Question

Commenting on John Marsh's assertion that Jesus made it plain that the Kingdom had already come, Millar Burrows suggested that

> If that is so, I submit, it is passing strange that Jesus told his disciples to pray, "Thy Kingdom come." Those who maintain that for Jesus himself the Kingdom of God had already come in his own person and ministry inevitably treat this second petition of the Lord's prayer in a rather cavalier fashion. It must be interpreted, they say, in line with other sayings of Jesus. Why? And what other sayings? When all the evidence in the sayings of Jesus for "realized eschatology" is thoroughly tested, it boils

---

[23]Kenneth W. Clark, "Realized Eschatology," *Journal of Biblical Literature* 59 (September 1940): 374.

[24]Tobit 8:1ff.

[25]Bultmann, *History of the Synoptic Tradition*, 14.

down to ἔφθασεν ἐφ' ὑμᾶς ["is come upon you"] of Matthew 12:28 and Luke 11:20. Why should that determine the interpretation of Matthew 6:10 and Luke 11:2? Why should a difficult, obscure saying establish the meaning of one that is clear and unambiguous?[26]

Burrows rightly contended that an obscure verse should not determine the meaning of unambiguous verses. Matthew 12:28 ‖ Luke 11:20 is an obscure, puzzling statement—Jesus' rejoinder to hostile critics who were accusing him of working in league with Beelzebul. Should problematic Matthew 12:28 ‖ Luke 11:20 be the hermeneutical cornerstone for interpreting the Kingdom? This question becomes acute when one notes that there are more than a hundred statements concerning the Kingdom of God in the Synoptics. The majority of these statements (see "Appendix I") present the Kingdom as a place, not an exorcistic power. The majority of these statements present the Kingdom as a future hope, not a present reality. Should the obvious meaning of these numerous statements be ignored in favor of the teaching of a difficult, obscure saying, namely, "the Kingdom of God has come upon you"? I believe this question should be answered in the negative.

Bearing upon this line of reasoning is an observation made by Professor Dodd: "I distinguish between exegesis of particular passages and interpretation in the wider sense."[27] Exegetes could march back and forth for years across Matthew 12:28 ‖ Luke 11:20, some defending Dodd's exegesis of this logion, others opposing Dodd's exegesis of this logion. If at some distant point in the future they should unanimously agree among themselves on what Matthew 12:28 ‖ Luke 11:20 means (a remote possibility indeed!) and if—for the sake of argument—they agreed Dodd's interpretation of this logion was right, this unanimous exegetical agreement would not deliver exegetes from the task of interpretation in the wider sense. When this wider interpretive task is undertaken, when all the evidence is considered, hermeneutical weight would have to be assigned to the scores of synoptic statements portraying the Kingdom as a future realm, rather than to Matthew 12:28 ‖ Luke 11:20 (which—according to Dodd—portrays the Kingdom as a curative power). Realized eschatologists reverse

---

[26]Millar Burrows, "Thy Kingdom Come," *Journal of Biblical Literature* (March 1955): 5.

[27]Dodd, *The Parables of the Kingdom*, vi.

this procedure. They assign hermeneutical weight to problematic Matthew 12:28 || Luke 11:20 and ignore the scores of statements portraying the Kingdom as a future realm.

These objections to Dodd's exegesis are decisive; how, therefore, can the Matthew 12:28 logion be understood? One must remember (as Claude C. Douglas demonstrated[28]) that Jesus frequently used hyperbole. If one bears in mind that Jesus used overstatement, it is possible to interpret Matthew 12:28 as a hyperbolic pronouncement of the imminence and certainty of the Kingdom's arrival. Jesus interpreted his skill at exorcism as a *proof* or as a *sign* that the *basileia* he proclaimed was an impending miracle. At any moment it was going to crash in upon the world of first-century Jewry!

Thus ἔφθασεν in Matthew 12:28 bears a force similar to the force it bears in 1 Thessalonians 2:16. In a context wherein he berated the Jews for crucifying Jesus and persecuting the Church, Paul wrote concerning the Jews, "But God's wrath comes [ἔφθασεν] upon them finally." The import of this statement is clear: with certainty the wrath of God will come upon those who have slain Jesus and persecuted his followers. Similarly, in Matthew 12:28 Jesus declared that the Kingdom's arrival was imminent. Of this fact his exorcisms were proof or guarantee. Such an interpretation would be the natural interpretation of the εἰ protasis and the ἄρα apodosis in Matthew 12:28. Thus Donald Joseph Selby was right in observing that

> The fundamental difficulty that appears in the hypothesis of "realized eschatology" lies in Dodd's failure to distinguish between the anticipating events and the *eschaton* itself. Is it not possible to understand the high pitch of expectance and hope that were admittedly present during the ministry of Jesus to mean that the guarantee of the *eschaton* was with them? That is to say, the preliminary events had begun to appear. But there seems to be no warrant for saying that the disciples believed that the "event" itself had yet arrived.[29]

To the point also is the observation of Martin Dibelius,

---

[28]Claude C. Douglas, *Overstatement in the New Testament* (New York: Henry Holt, 1931).

[29]Donald Joseph Selby, "Changing Ideas in New Testament Eschatology," *Harvard Theological Review* 50 (January 1957): 23.

"But if it is by the finger of God that I expel the evil spirits, then God's Kingdom has already made its presence known among you" (Luke 11:19, 20). In this saying too, whose wording permits the translation, "God's Kingdom has come even to you," it is not said that God's Kingdom is already there—of such a statement, these expulsions taken alone would really have been no proof!—but that in the abundance of such wonderful events it announced its proximity. Hence the demon expulsions are also signs of the coming Kingdom.[30]

In a word, Mr. Dodd confused premonitory signs of the Kingdom's imminence with the Kingdom's actual arrival.

2. The Message to John the Baptist
(Matthew 11:2-6 || Luke 7:18-23)

For Professor Dodd to use this pericope in explaining what the Kingdom of God means is curious because it does not contain the expression "Kingdom of God." Matthew 11:4-6 || Luke 7:22-23 is the synoptic account of John's disciples' visit with Jesus. The words emphasized by Dodd are:

And Jesus answered them, "Go and tell John what you hear and see: the blind receive their sight and the lame walk, lepers are cleansed and the deaf hear, and the dead are raised up, and the poor have good news preached to them. And blessed is he who takes no offense at me."
(Matthew 11:4-6)

In this statement Jesus was referring to the "mighty works" characterizing his career. This is made clear in the parallel Lukan account wherein the remark is added that "in that hour he cured many of diseases and plagues and evil spirits, and on many that were blind he bestowed sight" (Luke 7:21).

With reference to Jesus' reply to John's disciples, Dodd wrote:

Jesus points to the phenomena of His own ministry in terms which clearly allude to prophecies of the "good time coming." The implication is that the time of fulfilment has come: that which the prophets desired to see is now a matter of present experience. John is himself not merely one of the prophets, but greater than any prophet, because he is the Messenger

---

[30]Martin Dibelius, *Jesus*, trans. Charles B. Hedrick and Frederick C. Grant (Philadelphia: Westminster Press, 1939) 78-79.

of whom the prophets spoke, who should immediately precede the great divine event, the coming of the Kingdom of God. The implication is clear: John has played his destined part, and the Kingdom of God has come.[31]

Again Dodd implies that Jesus gave sight to blind eyes, restored hearing to deaf ears, imparted strength to the lame, cleansed lepers, raised the dead, and preached to the poor because the *basileia* as a curative power was active in him. An equation in Dodd's mind was: Jesus' healing miracles equals the Kingdom's arrival. Such a judgment, however, is not in keeping with the flow of synoptic thought: the Synoptists (as pointed out in the first part of this chapter) ascribed Jesus' capacity for healing to his endowment with *dunamis, exousia,* and *pneuma*. Since in this pericope (Matthew 11:4-6 || Luke 7:22-23) there is *no explicit statement* that the miracles witnessed by John's disciples (Luke 7:21) were performed through the *basileia* of God, it is logical to assume that these miracles (like Jesus' other miracles) were performed by *dunamis* or *exousia* or *pneuma* as agents of God's dynamic activity in Christ. Dodd again mixed New Testament categories; he confused *basileia* with *dunamis, exousia,* and *pneuma*.

The evidence suggests that Luke ascribed the miracles alluded to in Matthew 11:4-6 || Luke 7:22-23 to the activity of the *pneuma* of God. Such is the case because Jesus' reply to John's emissaries contained allusions to Isaiah 35:5-6 and 61:1-2. The latter of these passages is cited in the Third Gospel in the pericope (Luke 4:17-18) recounting the rejection of Jesus at Nazareth.

> And there was given to him the book of the prophet Isaiah. He opened the book and found the place where it was written, "The Spirit of the Lord is upon me, because he has annointed me to preach good news to the poor. He has sent me to proclaim release to the captives and recovering of sight to the blind, to set at liberty those who are oppressed."
> (Luke 4:17-18)

Here Jesus is presented as claiming to be annointed with the Spirit in order to preach good news to the poor and recovery of sight to the blind. If an exegete desired to ascribe the preaching to the poor and the recovery of sight (alluded to in Luke 7:22-23) to a particular agent of God's activity, he would at least be in keeping with Lucan theology to ascribe such activ-

---

[31]Dodd, *The Parables of the Kingdom*, 47.

ities to the *pneuma* of God and not to *basileia*. Thus nothing in Matthew 11:2-6, Luke 7:18-23 justifies Dodd's eisegetical judgment that Jesus' miracles per se were evidence the Kingdom had come.

3. The Markan Gospel Summary
(Mark 1:14-15)

> Now after John was arrested, Jesus came into Galilee, preaching the gospel of God, and saying, "The time is fulfilled, and the kingdom of God is at hand; repent, and believe in the gospel."   (Mark 1:14-15)

Krister Stendahl, with his knack for apt expression, once observed that a "battle of centimeters" has raged over the ἤγγικεν ("it comes/draws near") of Mark 1:15. How near *is* near in ἤγγικεν? Dodd argued in *The Parables of the Kingdom* that ἤγγικεν in Mark 1:15 had the same meaning as ἔφθασεν in Matthew 12:28.[32] His interpretation was immediately challenged because Dodd erred in citing LXX evidence. While citing LXX evidence in the first edition of *The Parables of the Kingdom,* Dodd wrote that

> In the LXX the perfect of the verb ἐγγίζειν is used to translate the Hebrew verb *naga* and the Aramaic verb *m'ta,* both of which mean "to reach," "to arrive." The same two verbs are also translated by the aorist of the verb φθάνειν, which is used in Matthew 12:28, Luke 11:20. It would appear therefore that no difference of meaning is intended between ἔφθασεν ἐφ' ὑμᾶς ἡ βασιλεία τοῦ θεοῦ, and ἤγγικεν ἡ βασιλεία τοῦ θεοῦ. Both imply the "arrival" of something which has hitherto been the object of expectation. We should translate both: "The Kingdom of God has come."[33]

---

[32]Only brief attention will be given to ἐγγίζω. Its meaning has been investigated numerous times, and there is little doubt that Dodd's interpretation of this verb was shown to be false. Note the following articles: Matthew Black, "The Kingdom of God Has Come," *Expository Times* 63 (June 1952): 289-90; Clarence T. Craig, "Realized Eschatology," *Journal of Biblical Literature* 56 (March 1937): 19-20; Kenneth W. Clark, "Realized Eschatology" *Journal of Biblical Literature* (September 1940): 367-74; J. Y. Campbell, "The Kingdom of God Has Come," *Expository Times* 48 (December 1936): 138-42; W. R. Hutton, "The Kingdom of God Has Come," *Expository Times* 64 (December 1952): 89-91; Reginald H. Fuller, *The Mission and Achievement of Jesus* (London: SCM Press Ltd., 1954) 20-25.

[33]Dodd, *The Parables of the Kingdom,* 44.

As J. Y. Campbell quickly pointed out, however, Professor Dodd was in error in his interpretation of LXX evidence. In a critique of Dodd's exegesis Campbell wrote,

> There are only seven certain occurrences of the perfect of the verb ἐγγίζειν in the LXX. In none of these does it translate either *naga* or *m'ta;* in all the six instances where the Hebrew is extant it translates some form of the root *qarab*, which means "to come near, to approach." In Jeremiah 51:9 (LXX 28:9), where the Hebrew is *naga*, the Vatican manuscript (B) has the perfect, but the Sinaitic (S) and Alexandrine (A) manuscripts have the aorist. The aorist has internal probability in its favor, since the verb in the parallel clause is in the aorist, and has the support of Rahlfs in his recent edition of the LXX.[34]

Thus Dodd's argument that ἤγγικεν and ἔφθασεν are synonymous in meaning because in the LXX they translate the same verbs was false. In an ineffectual rebuttal to Campbell's article, Dodd admitted he had tried to make ἤγγικεν conform in meaning to ἔφθασεν. "I take ἔφθασεν at its face value, and try to make ἤγγικεν conform."[35] This is a dubious exegetical procedure. After Campbell's criticisms had been published in *The Expository Times*, Dodd corrected his error but changed the wording so slightly that his discussion (see page 44 of *The Parables of the Kingdom;* 29 in the 1961 rev. ed.) gives a false impression to an unsuspecting reader. Dodd had no substantial reason to argue from the LXX that ἤγγικεν and ἔφθασεν are synonymous in meaning.

Dodd's interpretation of ἤγγικεν breaks down when the use of this verb in Matthew 3:2 is considered.[36] John the Baptist is presented in Matthew 3:2 as proclaiming, "Repent, for the kingdom of Heaven has drawn near (ἤγγικεν)." Regardless of whether one does or does not believe that John proclaimed the Kingdom of God, few exegetes would argue that for the Synoptists the Kingdom arrived (or was "realized") with John the

---

[34]Campbell, "The Kingdom of God Has Come," 91-92.

[35]Dodd, "The Kingdom of God Has Come," *The Expository Times* 48 (December 1936): 138.

[36]The Synoptics teach that the Kingdom was *near*, not that it had actually arrived. It should be noted that on page 48 of *The Parables of the Kingdom* Dodd argued that in Matthew 3:2 the author of the First Gospel has "mistakenly attributed words of Jesus to the Baptist." That the Baptist *did* proclaim the Kingdom, however, is obvious from Luke 16:16.

Baptist. Yet this would be the meaning of Matthew 3:2 if Dodd's interpretation of ἤγγικεν is correct. Thus Mark 1:14-15 is fragile evidence on which to base a hypothesis that the Kingdom was inaugurated in Jesus.

4. The Beatitude of Hearing and Seeing (Matthew 13:16-17 ‖ Luke 10:23-24)

With reference to the Beatitude of Hearing and Seeing (a beatitude that does *not* contain the expression "Kingdom of God") Dodd wrote,

> There are other passages in our oldest Gospel sources which help to make it clear that Jesus intended to proclaim the Kingdom of God not as something to come in the near future, but as a matter of present experience. "Blessed are the eyes that see what you see; for I tell you that many prophets and kings wished to see what you see, and did not see it, and to hear what you hear and did not hear it" (Luke 10:23-24, and with insignificant variation, Matthew 13:16-17). That which prophets and kings (such as David the psalmist, and Solomon, to whom the Messianic "Psalms of Solomon" were attributed) desired, is naturally to be understood as the final assertion of God's sovereignty in the world, the coming of "the Kingdom of God." This it is what the disciples of Jesus "see and hear."[37]

Dodd failed to point out, however, that the Beatitude of Hearing and Seeing appears in Matthew and Luke in different contexts. It was a floating tradition, and to determine its original reference is impossible. In Luke the beatitude has no connection with its context; it immediately follows the "Johannine" pronouncement of Jesus (Luke 10:21-22) and immediately precedes the two-fold summary of the Law (Luke 10:25-28). In this Lukan context there is no reference to the Kingdom of God, and Dodd's suggestion that the Lukan beatitude referred to the *basileia* was arbitrary.

The Beatitude of Hearing and Seeing in Matthew 13:16-17 does have a relationship to its context. One problem faced by early Christian apologists was: Why had Israel refused to accept Jesus as Messiah? Why had the call to repentance proclaimed by John and Jesus had only transitory influence on the mass of Jews? The response of primitive Christian apologetic to this problem was (to use B. W. Bacon's phrase) the doctrine of "the Hiding of the Revelation."

---

[37] Dodd, *The Parables of the Kingdom*, 46.

88 • Rethinking Realized Eschatology

This doctrine makes its initial appearance in Paul. In Romans 9-11, which is devoted to explaining Israel's displacement by the Church as God's agent, Paul resorted to the complaint of Isaiah (Isaiah 6:10) as follows,

> Israel failed to obtain what it sought. The elect obtained it, but the rest were hardened, as it is written, "God gave them a spirit of stupor, eyes that should not see and ears that should not hear, down to this very day."
> (Romans 11:7-8)

It was in terms of the Isaian prediction of the Deaf Ear and Blind Eye with which Israel greeted the prophet's message that Paul interpreted the Jewish refusal to accept Jesus as Messiah. In Israel's rejection of the Gospel (so Paul thought) was a fulfillment of the Isaian prediction about deaf ears and blind eyes.

Mark attempts to support this primitive apologetic about the Hiding of the Revelation with a saying of Jesus.

> And he said to them, "To you has been given the secret of the kingdom of God, but for those outside everything is in parables; so that they may indeed see but not perceive, and may indeed hear but not understand; lest they should turn again, and be forgiven." (Mark 4:11-12 ‖ Luke 8:10)

Mark believed Jesus taught in such a way that

> he met the obduracy of his kindred after the flesh by a method of teaching such that only they who had "ears to hear" received "the mystery of the Kingdom," whereas the "outsiders" had fulfilled to them the Isaian prediction.[38]

This puzzling theory "that parables are enigmas and that Jesus used these transparent illustrations to veil his message from his kindred after the flesh while revealing it to the select group of his disciples"[39] has a prominent place in Mark.

In Matthew 13:10-17 the evangelist used this same theodicy. In response to the disciples' question regarding the purpose of parables, Jesus is represented as saying,

---

[38]Benjamin W. Bacon, *Studies in Matthew* (New York: Henry Holt, 1930) 382.
[39]Ibid.

This is why I speak to them in parables, because seeing they do not see, and hearing they do not hear, nor do they understand. With them indeed is fulfilled the prophecy of Isaiah which says: "You shall indeed hear but never understand, and you shall indeed see but never perceive. For this people's heart has grown dull, and their ears are heavy of hearing, and their eyes they have closed, lest they should perceive with their eyes, and hear with their ears, and understand with their heart, and turn for me to heal them." But blessed are your eyes, for they see, and your ears, for they hear. Truly, I say to you, many prophets and righteous men longed to see what you see, and did not see it, and to hear what you hear, and did not hear it. (Matthew 13:10-17)

Recognizing in the Beatitude of Hearing and Seeing (Matthew 13:16-17) an appropriate means of contrasting the status of Jesus' enlightened disciples with the status of the unenlightened crowds, Matthew pragmatically inserted it after his citation of the Isaian prophecy about blind eyes and deaf ears. Thus Matthew 13:16-17 refers to the disciples of Jesus who, in contrast to the hardened multitude, have the ability (eyes that see and ears that hear) to understand Jesus' parables.[40] Because Jesus' disciples understood the parables, they knew secrets about his preaching (Matthew 13:11) that the multitudes did not know. Nothing in the Matthean Beatitude of Hearing and Seeing warrants Dodd's contention that for Jesus the *basileia* had arrived. The beatitude occurs in a pericope (Matthew 13:10-17) that is a primitive Christian apologetic and that has nothing to do with the Kingdom of God. For Dodd to build his theory of realized eschatology on a saying like Matthew 13:16-17 || Luke 10:23-24 suggests how hard pressed he was for supporting biblical data.

5. The Men of Nineveh and Queen of the South Condemnation (Matthew 12:41-42 || Luke 11:31-32)

The men of Nineveh will arise at the judgment with this generation and condemn it; for they repented at the preaching of Jonah, and behold, something greater than Jonah is here. The queen of the South will arise

---

[40]This is the interpretation followed by most biblical commentators. Note, e.g., Theodore H. Robinson, *The Gospel of Matthew* (New York: Harper and Brothers, 1927) 120; Alan Hugh M'Neile, *The Gospel According to St. Matthew* (London: Macmillan, 1952) 192.

at the judgment with this generation and condemn it; for she came from the ends of the earth to hear the wisdom of Solomon, and behold, something greater than Solomon is here. (Matthew 12:41-42)

With reference to this Jonah-Solomon pericope (which does *not* contain the expression "Kingdom of God"), Dodd wrote, "What is this 'something greater' than Jonah the prophet and Solomon the wise king? Surely it is that which prophets and kings desired to see, the coming of the Kingdom of God."[41] This suggestion by Dodd that the "something greater" referred to in the Jonah-Solomon comparison is the Kingdom of God is a conjecture on his part. Nothing in the pericope demands (or suggests) this interpretation.[42] The usual interpretation of Matthew 12:41-42 is that it refers to the life and ministry of Jesus.[43] Dodd protested this traditional interpretation on the grounds that neuter *pleion* (πλεῖον) could not be translated "a greater than Solomon," for such a translation would demand a masculine adjective. However, if Dodd desired to be fastidious about grammar, it should be observed that *pleion* cannot refer to *basileia*. *Basileia* is feminine and would require a feminine adjective.

A much more probable interpretation of Matthew 12:41-42 is that of B. W. Bacon who suggested that the Jonah-Solomon comparison deals with Israel's rejection of God's two messengers: "John's warning of judgment being compared to Jonah's at Nineveh and Jesus' winning entreaty to the wisdom of Solomon."[44] If Bacon's conjecture is correct, there is a similarity between Matthew 12:41-42 and Matthew 11:16-19.

> But to what shall I compare this generation? It is like children sitting in the market places and calling to their playmates, "We piped to you, and you did not dance; we wailed, and you did not mourn." For John came neither eating nor drinking, and they say, "He has a demon"; the Son of man came eating and drinking, and they say, "Behold, a glutton and a

---

[41]Dodd, *The Parables of the Kingdom,* 46-47.

[42]Though, to be sure, Dodd's interpretation has been widely adopted in English theological circles. Note, e.g., H. D. A. Major, T. W. Manson, C. J. Wright, *The Mission and Message of Jesus* (New York: E. P. Dutton, 1938) 384.

[43]M'Neile, *The Gospel According to St. Matthew* 182; Robinson, *The Gospel of Matthew,* 115.

[44]Bacon, *Studies in Matthew,* 383.

drunkard, a friend of tax collectors and sinners!'' Yet wisdom is justified by her deeds. (Matthew 11:16-19)

In both pericopes Jews are condemned for rejecting John's and Jesus' message. Both reflect a Wisdom Christology, for in Matthew 12:42 Jesus is compared to Solomon and in Matthew 11:19 Jesus is expressly referred to as *sophia* ("yet *sophia* is justified by her deeds").

6. The Violence Remark
(Matthew 11:12-13 || Luke 16:16)

The logion contrasting the Law and Prophets with the Kingdom of God appears in the Synoptics in two forms.

> From the days of John the Baptist until now the kingdom of heaven has suffered violence, and men of violence take it by force. For all the prophets and the law prophesied until John. (Matthew 11:12-13)

> The law and the prophets were until John; since then the good news of the kingdom of God is preached, and every one enters it violently.
> (Luke 16:16)

Even a casual reading reveals nothing in these statements to substantiate Dodd's thesis that the *basileia* was an abstract power operative in Jesus' ministry. Dodd candidly admitted that "the original form of the saying, and its precise meaning, are exceedingly difficult to determine."[45] Moreover, in the preface to the third edition of *The Parables of the Kingdom*, he conceded that Matthew 11:12-13 "is a notorious *crux interpretum*,[46] and I am not at all sure that I understand it."[47]

Both the Matthean and the Lukan form of the logion seem to conceive of John as "the hinge upon which history turns."[48] Prior to John were the Law and the Prophets; after John is the proclamation of the Kingdom of

---

[45] Dodd, *The Parables of the Kingdom*, 48.

[46] The difficulty in reaching a meaningful understanding of this logion can be seen in the following articles: Frederick W. Danker, "Luke 16:16—An Opposition Logion," *Journal of Biblical Literature* 77 (September 1958): 231-43; J. Hugh Michael, "A Conjecture on Matthew 11:12," *Harvard Theological Review* 14 (October 1921): 375-76.

[47] Dodd, *The Parables of the Kingdom*, 3rd ed. (London: James Nisbet and Company, 1936) v.

[48] M'Neile, *The Gospel According to St. Matthew*, 156.

God. Matthew 11:12 is probably to be understood as a condemnation of revolutionaries like Judas of Galilee who attempted by force to bring in the Golden Age of the Jewish people.[49] But βιάζω ("is pressing," "enters [it] violently") in Luke 16:16 has a different subject (πᾶς, "every one," "all"), and to be sure of its meaning in this anomalous verse is impossible. However, one insight is clear: neither in Matthew 11:12-13 nor in Luke 16:16 is there evidence suggesting the *basileia* was "realized" in the ministry of Jesus.

III. The Parables of the Kingdom

In the Synoptics, eleven parables are referred explicitly to the Kingdom of God. These parables are the Mustard Seed (Mark 4:30-32 ‖ Luke 13:18-19 ‖ Matthew 13:31-32), the Seed Growing Secretly (Mark 4:26-29), the Leaven (Matthew 13:33 ‖ Luke 13:20-21), the Hid Treasure (Matthew 13:44), the Pearl (Matthew 13:45), the Great Feast (Matthew 22:1-13 ‖ Luke 14:16-24), the Ten Virgins (Matthew 25:1-12), the Weeds (Matthew 13:24-30, 36-43), the Fishnet (Matthew 13:47-50), the Unforgiving Servant (Matthew 18:23-35), and the Vineyard Workers (Matthew 20:1-16). With reference to the parable of the Great Feast in Luke 14:16-24, it should be noted that it is not explicitly referred to the Kingdom, but Luke 14:15 implies such a reference.

In *The Parables of the Kingdom* Dodd interpreted these eleven parables in accordance with his hypothesis that the *basileia* was operative in Jesus. It was his contention that explicit statements (the six passages noted in the preceding section) in the Synoptics dealing with the Kingdom taught that the *basileia* was present in Jesus. Therefore, the parables of Jesus (so Dodd argued) should be interpreted in the light of this explicit teaching.

In the discussion that follows, I shall not attempt a detailed explication of the Kingdom parables. Rather, I intend to examine the eleven Kingdom parables to determine what light they throw upon two crucial problems for Professor Dodd's hypothesis of realized eschatology. The first problem is: Do the Kingdom parables portray the Kingdom as present or as future? The second problem is: Do the Kingdom parables portray the Kingdom as an abstract, curative power or as a place?

---

[49]Ibid., 155.

1. Interpreted Kingdom Parables

The parable of the Weeds (Matthew 13:24-30) and the parable of the Fishnet (Matthew 13:47-50) are the two Kingdom parables transmitted with interpretations. Both parables, Hans Conzelmann contends, emphasize the *futurity* of the Kingdom.[50] The Weed parable is interpreted in Matthew as follows:

> Then he left the crowds and went into the house. And his disciples came to him, saying, "Explain to us the parable of the weeds of the field." He answered, "He who sows the good seed is the son of man; the field is the world, and the good seed means the sons of the kingdom; the weeds are the sons of the evil one, and the enemy who sowed them is the devil; the harvest is the close of the age, and reapers are angels. Just as the weeds are gathered and burned with fire, so will it be at the close of the age. The son of man will send his angels, and they will gather out of his kingdom all causes of sin and all evildoers, and throw them into the furnace of fire; there men will weep and gnash their teeth. Then the righteous will shine like the sun in the kingdom of their Father." (Matthew 13:36-43)

Nothing in this interpretation supports Dodd's hypothesis of realized eschatology. However, much points *against* Dodd's hypothesis. In this interpretation the close of the age, the judgment, and the expulsion of evildoers from the Kingdom are juxtaposed. This juxtaposition suggests that the close of the age and the Kingdom's arrival coincide. Thus the Kingdom's arrival is conceived to be a future occurrence. Moreover, in the interpretation, the Kingdom is presented in spatial terms. Angels will gather out of the Kingdom the evildoers and will cast them into a furnace of fire (Matthew 13:41-42). After this expulsion the sons of the Kingdom will shine like the sun in the Kingdom of their father (Matthew 13:43).

In many parabolic discussions it is in fashion to view the Weed parable's interpretation as secondary. Concerning its interpretation Dodd wrote,

> The interpretation indeed which Matthew has annexed is even more obviously secondary than the Marcan interpretation of the Sower, by which it was probably suggested.[51] . . . We shall do well to forget this interpretation as completely as possible.[52]

---

[50]Hans Conzelmann, *Jesus* (Philadelphia: Fortress Press, 1973) 72-74.

[51]Dodd, *The Parables of the Kingdom,* 183.

[52]Ibid., 184.

A similar opinion has been expressed by A. T. Cadoux,[53] Joachim Jeremias,[54] and B. T. D. Smith.[55] To understand why exegetes are anxious to disparage the Weed parable interpretation is not difficult. This interpretation portrays Jesus as having a spatial understanding of the Kingdom, as believing angels will forcibly remove evildoers from the Kingdom and cast them into a furnace of fire, and as believing that after this expulsion the righteous will shine with a heavenly radiance. By viewing Matthew 13:36-43 as secondary, it is possible to avoid the position that Jesus held these "curious" beliefs.

However, the brusque dismissal of the parable's interpretation as nothing more than the handiwork of the primitive Church is an exegetical tour de force of dubious value. Such a dismissal assumes the early Church misunderstood Jesus. The hypothesis that the early Church misunderstood Jesus is not an attractive hypothesis for the obvious reason that our knowledge about Jesus is dependent upon the Church's transmission of traditions about him. If, however, the early Church (because of obtuseness or because of Jesus' mediocre pedagogic abilities) misunderstood Jesus, then with reference to Jesus' thought an attitude of agnosticism must prevail. If the image of Jesus transmitted by the Church is a false, distorted image, then present-day understanding of Jesus will also be false and distorted. It is impossible through imagination or conjecture to penetrate behind the image of Jesus that the early Church has given.

The parable of the Fishnet is found in Matthew 13:47-50:

> Again, the kingdom of heaven is like a net which was thrown into the sea and gathered fish of every kind; when it was full, men drew it ashore and sat down and sorted the good into vessels but threw away the bad. So it will be at the close of the age. The angels will come and separate the evil from the righteous, and throw them into the furnace of fire; there men will weep and gnash their teeth.

---

[53] A. T. Cadoux, *The Parables of Jesus* (London: James Clarke and Company, 1931) 29.

[54] Joachim Jeremias, *The Parables of Jesus*, trans. S. H. Hooke (New York: Charles Scribner's Sons, 1955) 67.

[55] B. T. D. Smith, *The Parables of the Synoptic Gospels* (Cambridge: Cambridge University Press, 1937) 200.

The teaching of the Fishnet parable is similar to the Weed parable. In both appears the physical expulsion of the unrighteous from the Kingdom; in both appears the idea that the Kingdom's arrival coincides with the close of the age.

Thus the two interpreted Kingdom parables present the Kingdom as a future hope and as a realm or place.[56] These interpretations are inimical to the conception of an abstract, present Kingdom advocated by Professor Dodd.

2. Noninterpreted Kingdom Parables

Nine Kingdom parables appear in the Synoptics without interpretation. They are the parables of the Mustard Seed, the Seed Growing Secretly, the Leaven, the Hid Treasure, the Pearl, the Great Feast, the Ten Virgins, the Unforgiving Servant, and the Vineyard Workers. The noninterpreted parables are of no help in determining whether the evangelists conceived of the Kingdom in abstract or spatial terms. The Kingdom parables do not define the Kingdom; rather, they speak of what the Kingdom is *like*. An exegete in dealing with noninterpreted Kingdom parables is confronted with the hermeneutical problem: *it is impossible to argue with certainty from a comparison.*[57] For example, the parable of the Hidden

---

[56] From Matthew 13:19 one could argue that the parable of the Sower was an interpreted Kingdom parable, but in Matthew 13:1-9 it is not explicitly referred to the Kingdom. It is to be noted, however, that in Matthew 13:19 (as in Matthew 4:23; 9:35; 24:14) the Kingdom is presented as the object of a proclamation.

[57] The following are the comparative statements that appear in noninterpreted Kingdom parables:

(1) Mark 4:26 And he said, "The kingdom of God is as if a man should scatter seed upon the ground."
(2) Mark 4:30-31a And he said, "With what can we compare the kingdom of God, or what parable shall we use for it? It is like a grain of mustard seed."
(3) Matthew 13:31 Another parable he put before them, saying, "The kingdom of heaven is like a grain of mustard seed which a man took and sowed in his field." (Note parallel in Luke 13:18-19a.)
(4) Matthew 13:33a "The kingdom of heaven is like leaven which a woman took and hid in three measures of meal, till it was all leavened." (Note parallel in Luke 13:20-21.)
(5) Matthew 13:44a "The kingdom of heaven is like treasure hidden in a field, which a man found and covered up."
(6) Matthew 13:45 "Again, the kingdom of heaven is like a merchant in search of fine pearls."
(7) Matthew 18:23 "Therefore the kingdom of heaven may be compared to a king who

Treasure in all probability teaches that the Kingdom is of immense value. However, this assertion could be made with equal force concerning a spatial or an abstract Kingdom. Thus the noninterpreted Kingdom parables are of no help in determining whether Jesus conceived of the Kingdom in spatial or abstract terms. Neither are they of help in determining whether the Kingdom was viewed by Jesus as a present reality or a future hope.

IV. Conclusion

New Testament evidence for Dodd's Kingdom version of realized eschatology does not exist. When the six crucial passages, "the most explicit of their kind," used by Professor Dodd as a scriptural basis for realized eschatology are subjected to examination, this conclusion emerges: serious objections can be raised against all six passages. Three of them do not contain the phrase "Kingdom of God." A fourth (Matthew 11:12-13 ‖ Luke 16:16) was labeled by Professor Dodd "a notorious *crux interpretum*." His interpretation of a fifth passage (Mark 1:14-15) revolved around an erroneous use of LXX data. The sixth passage (Matthew 12:28 ‖ Luke 11:20) is a problematic retort Jesus made to critics. Moreover, the interpreted Kingdom parables point against Dodd's hypothesis. I repeat an opinion expressed previously in this chapter: Professor Dodd's Kingdom version of realized eschatology is a hermeneutical castle built upon exegetical quicksand.

The view expressed in the previous paragraph, however, is mine. Turn again to "Appendix I," below, and read reflectively all the statements in the Synoptics containing the word *Kingdom*. As you read them, appealing to your own analytical powers, ask yourself: How many of these statements present the Kingdom as a curative power responsible for Jesus' exorcisms? How many harmonize with Professor Dodd's Kingdom version of realized eschatology? To my mind the answer is obvious: none of them harmonize with Professor Dodd's Kingdom version of realized eschatology.

---

    wished to settle accounts with his servants."
(8) Matthew 20:1 "For the kingdom of heaven is like a householder who went out early in the morning to hire laborers for his vineyard."
(9) Matthew 22:2 "The kingdom of heaven may be compared to a king who gave a marriage feast for his son."
(10) Matthew 25:1 "Then the kingdom of heaven shall be compared to ten maidens who took their lamps and went out to meet the bridegroom."

Appended Note
Do Rudolf Otto and Gustaf Dalman Support Dodd's Hermeneutics?

In *The Parables of the Kingdom* Dodd appealed to both Rudolf Otto and Gustaf Dalman for support of his abstract interpretation of *basileia*. Both of these men were giants in the field of New Testament studies, and their support of Dodd's thesis would be of no small significance. In this appended note I raise the question: Do Otto and Dalman *in fact* support Dodd in his abstract interpretation of the Kingdom of God? Attention will first of all be given to Otto's *The Kingdom of God and the Son of Man*.

It is true that Otto argued that the *basileia* was operative in Jesus as *dunamis*,[58] and that it "penetrated from the future into the present" (whatever this means).[59] But Otto, in contrast to Dodd, gave attention to *all* the New Testament evidence. Dodd in *The Parables of the Kingdom* reduced the *basileia* to an abstract power; Otto inconsistently argued it was both a *power* operative in Jesus and a *realm*. Yet from reading *The Parables of the Kingdom* one would never suspect that Otto possessed this latter conception. Dodd in his quoting of Otto was a master of ex parte quotation. For example, Dodd wrote,

> Whatever we make of them, the sayings which declare the Kingdom of God to have come are explicit and unequivocal. . . . If therefore we are seeking the *differentia* of the teaching of Jesus upon the Kingdom of God, it is here that it must be found.[60]

This just-quoted statement was footnoted by Dodd as follows.

> Among recent writers the one who does fullest justice to this idea is Rudolf Otto. His phrase for it is "der Schonanbruch des Reiches Gottes." I cannot see how anyone, after reading *Reich Gottes und Menschensohn*, pp. 51-73, could ever be content with interpretations which water down the meaning of these great sayings into a mere expectation that the Kingdom of God would come very soon.[61]

---

[58]Rudolf Otto, *The Kingdom of God and the Son of Man*, trans. Floyd V. Filson and Bertram Lee-Woolf (London: Lutterworth Press, 1943) 44.

[59]Ibid., 72.

[60]Dodd, *The Parables of the Kingdom*, 49.

[61]Ibid.

A close reading of Otto's book, however, will reveal scores of places where he conceived of the kingdom both in *spatial terms* and as a *future hope*.[62] Thus Dodd's appeal to Otto carried connotations that a reading of *The Kingdom of God and the Son of Man* will reveal are not justified.

In contending that *basileia* in the New Testament was an abstract noun, Dodd also appealed to Gustaf Dalman's *Die Worte Jesu* for support of his interpretation.[63] In a context wherein he argued that *basileia* meant "reign" or "sovereignty" because it represented the Jewish term *malkuth*, Dodd footnoted his discussion as follows.

> "There can be no doubt," says Dalman, "that in the O.T. as in Jewish literature, *malkuth* as related to God always means 'kingly rule' and never 'Kingdom'." It seems best, however, to retain the traditional expression, "The Kingdom of God," bearing in mind that the word *Kingdom* carries in this case the sense of "kingly rule."[64]

Observing that Dodd cited Dalman as his authority in this strategic part of *The Parables of the Kingdom*, a reader would infer that Dalman (like Dodd) believed that *basileia* in the Synoptics had an abstract significance ("kingly rule"). However, a perusal of Dalman's discussion will show that repeatedly he argued that for Jesus the *basileia* was a theocracy.[65] Dalman pointed out, for example, the similarity between Jesus' concept of feasting in the Messianic Age and the concept of feasting found in apocalyptic literature.[66] Moreover, Dalman concluded his discussion by explicitly stating that *basileia* in the Synoptics was not to be interpreted so much in terms of *malkuth* as in terms of the Age to Come.

> The parallels . . . from the Jewish literature have proved that the true affinity of the idea of the sovereignty of God, as taught by Jesus, is to be found not so much in the Jewish conception of שָׁמַיִם מַלְכוּת as in the idea of the "future age" (הָעוֹלָם הַבָּא). . . . The "sovereignty of God" is for

---

[62]Otto, *The Kingdom of God and the Son of Man*, 25-31, 36-38, 48-54.

[63]Dodd, *The Parables of the Kingdom*, 34-36.

[64]Ibid., 34.

[65]Gustaf Dalman, *The Words of Jesus*, trans. D. M. Kay (Edinburgh: T. & T. Clark, 1902) 113, 114, 115, 116, 118, 119, 121, 122, 123, 125, 126, 127, 128, 133.

[66]Ibid., 110-11.

Jesus invariably an eschatological entity. . . . Independently of the schools and of the apocalyptic literature of His time, He created His own terminology. We may assume that He borrowed the term "sovereignty of God" as an eschatological designation from the Book of Daniel.[67]

Dalman considered *basileia* an eschatological term, but one would never suspect this from the way Dodd quoted *Die Worte Jesu*. Thus the purpose of this appended note is to protest Dodd's practice of ex parte quotation. Unintentionally the impression was created in *The Parables of the Kingdom* that Dodd's interpretation of *basileia* was supported both by Dalman and Otto. This is *not* the case.

---

[67]Ibid., 135-36.

CHAPTER
• 5 •

The Christological Version of Realized Eschatology

Up to this point in our study we have given attention to realized eschatology as developed by C. H. Dodd in *The Parables of the Kingdom,* that is, as a phrase designating the view that the Kingdom of God was a curative power operative in Jesus. In *The Parables of the Kingdom,* "realized eschatology" and the "Kingdom of God" are correlatives; you cannot speak of one without suggesting the other. Moreover, it is in this sense that most theologians and New Testament scholars use the expression "realized eschatology." I have labeled this use the "Kingdom version" of realized eschatology. (I am not certain the label is felicitous.) Scholars use this "Kingdom version" when "exegeting" the Synoptics and "explaining" what Jesus meant by the Kingdom of God. They use this version when "disproving" Johannes Weiss or Albert Schweitzer and when grappling with the issue of *explicatio* (explicating Jesus' teachings in their first-century context).

In his writings subsequent to 1935, however, Professor Dodd employed the phrase "realized eschatology" in discussions wherein he made no reference at all to the Kingdom of God. Consider, for example, his well-known work entitled *The Apostolic Preaching and Its Developments.* In this book, Professor Dodd, having analyzed the content of the primitive *kerygma,* asserted that the "earliest preaching" of the Church had the character of "realized eschatology."[1] Or consider his presidential address

---

[1]C. H. Dodd, *The Apostolic Preaching and Its Developments* (London: Hodder & Stoughton, 1936; New York: Harper and Brothers, ᵀᴾ1964, 1937) 39.

to the Oxford Society of Historical Theology. Having discussed in this address a number of verses containing no references to the Kingdom of God (Acts 2:16, 2 Corinthians 5:17, Titus 3:5, 1 Peter 1:23, 1 John 2:8), Dodd deduced from these passages that the Gospel of primitive Christianity was a "Gospel of realized eschatology."[2] Clearly in these statements "realized eschatology" bears a meaning other than the meaning it carries in *The Parables of the Kingdom*. Consequently, in this chapter I will argue that in his writings published after 1935 Professor Dodd used "realized eschatology" to designate the *significance* (meaning) *of the Christ event*. In the discussion that follows attention will be given to Professor Dodd's *The Apostolic Preaching and Its Developments, History and the Gospel, Gospel and Law, According to the Scriptures,* and *The Bible Today.* These books supplement one another, and taken together they afford another view of Dodd's hypothesis of realized eschatology. The view presented by Professor Dodd in these post-1935 publications can be labeled a *Christological version* of realized eschatology. Scholars use this Christological version when grappling with the issue of *applicatio* (applying Jesus' teachings and life to the contemporary situation).

I. A Preliminary Observation

In the nomenclature of theology the word *eschatology* means "the doctrine of the Last Things."[3] As traditionally understood, the term has temporal connotations and encompasses such matters as the last judgment, the resurrection, the end of the present world order, and the hope of life after death. Although in numerous instances Professor Dodd used *eschatology* in this traditional, temporal sense, nonetheless in other instances he used *eschatology* in a nontemporal, quasi-Platonic sense. If Dodd's use of "realized eschatology" to designate the *significance* of the Christ event is

---

[2]Ibid., 85.

[3]A helpful discussion of biblical eschatology, written by Ernst Jenni, Martin Rist, and John Wick Bowman, is found on pp. 126-40 of vol. E-J of *The Interpreter's Dictionary of the Bible* (Nashville: Abingdon Press, 1962); these articles deal with eschatological beliefs encountered in the Old Testament, Apocrypha and Pseudepigrapha, and New Testament. An updated discussion of current research regarding N.T. eschatology by E. Schüssler Fiorenza appears in the IDB supplementary volume (1976) on pp. 271-77. A much more concise introduction to biblical eschatology by Richard H. Hiers may be found on pp. 275-77 of *Harper's Bible Dictionary,* ed. Paul J. Achtemeier et al. (San Francisco: Harper & Row, 1985).

to be understood, we must be aware that in English theological circles the practice developed during the 1930s and 1940s of using *eschatology* to designate *that which is ultimate in significance rather than that which is ultimate in time.* Undoubtedly Dodd was one of the theologians responsible for this development. A meaningful discussion of this distinctive English usage is found in an article by C. K. Barrett in the *Scottish Journal of Theology*. Having noted the meaning of *eschatology* as used in mainstream Christian thought, that is, a temporal term referring to the Last Things, Barrett observed,

> This use of the word remains of course in current usage; but in modern biblical discussion *eschatology* is commonly employed in a somewhat different way, which may be defined by the statement that in characteristically eschatological thinking the *significance* of a series of events in time is defined in terms of the last of their number. The last event is not merely one member of the series; it is the determinative member which reveals the *meaning of the whole.*[4] . . . It is clear that any chain of events that can be thought of as closed may be regarded eschatologically; it makes no difference whether some or all of the events have actually taken place, provided that the last event whether past or future, is regarded as decisive.[5]

The discussion that follows will make clear that it was in this nontemporal sense—to denote that which is ultimate in meaning or significance—that Dodd used *eschatology* when he spoke of the Christ event as "realized eschatology" or as "eschatological fact."

II. Realized Eschatology as a Term to Denote the Significance of the Christ Event

1. Dodd's Philosophy of History

An analysis of Professor Dodd's concept of history is the necessary starting point for understanding his Christological version of realized es-

---

[4]C. K. Barrett, "New Testament Eschatology," *Scottish Journal of Theology* 16 (June 1953): 136; italics added.

[5]Ibid., 137. In regard to the qualitative use of *eschatology* and *eschaton* the following articles should be noted: C. C. McCown, "Symbolic Interpretation," *Journal of Biblical Literature* 63 (December 1944): 329-38; Clarence T. Craig, "Realized Eschatology," *Journal of Biblical Literature* 56 (March 1937): 17-26. The perplexity that naturally results from an unawareness of Dodd's nontemporal use of *eschatology* can be seen in A. W. Argyle's "Does Realized Eschatology Make Sense?" *Hibbert Journal* 51 (July 1953): 385-87.

chatology. Dodd observed that the word *history* has two distinct meanings. "It means both the course of events, and a record of the course of events."[6] This ambiguity is understandable because history consists of *remembered* events. Not everything that occurs is a historical event; only those occurrences that possess a certain intensity of meaning are retained in the corporate memory of a community.

Thus it follows, Professor Dodd suggested, that every historical event has two aspects—occurrence and meaning. *Occurrence plus meaning constitute a historical event.*[7] What Dodd meant by this formula (occurrence plus meaning equals historical event) can be illustrated by the Battle of Concord, the first battle of the American revolution. As far as occurrence is concerned, certain facts can be cited: British regulars, sent to Concord to destroy military supplies, were routed in battle by a militia of five hundred minutemen. Yet a reciting of these bare occurrences does not do full justice to what happened on 19 April 1775. Rather, attention must be given to the *meaning* of the Battle of Concord; it was the first military engagement of the American Revolutionary War and revealed the colonists' depth of feeling and their determination to fight for political independence. Only when attention is given to both *occurrence* and *meaning* is it possible to understand fully the *historical event* in which the "shot heard round the world" was fired.

Not only is every historical event composed of both occurrence and meaning, but Dodd also argued that historical events have varying intensities of meaning.[8] For example, the presidency of Warren G. Harding from 1921 through 1923 was a historical event with a certain intensity of meaning, but it did not have the intensity of meaning resident in the presidency of Abraham Lincoln or Woodrow Wilson or Franklin Delano Roosevelt. Later in this chapter it will become clear that this argument with regard to varying degrees of meaning resident in historical events is important in understanding Dodd's contention that the Christ event is an eschatological fact.

The conception of a historical event as occurrence plus meaning was used by Dodd as a frame of reference from which to understand the biblical

---

[6] C. H. Dodd, *The Bible Today* (Cambridge: Cambridge University Press, 1956) 99; *History and the Gospel* (London: James Nisbet and Company, 1938) 26.

[7] Dodd, *The Bible Today*, 99; *History and the Gospel*, 27, 36, 104.

[8] Dodd, *History and the Gospel*, 29.

revelation of God. Over against secular history (which seemingly is nothing more than the interplay of the contingent and the unforeseen[9]), man is confronted in the biblical revelation with *Heilsgeschichte* or "sacred history." Why the "fateful destiny" of playing a strategic role in *Heilsgeschichte* should have been entrusted to the Jewish nation is a problem that cannot be explained. In regard to this "scandal of particularity" Dodd wrote,

> We cannot pretend to explain *why* the fateful destiny of hearing the Word of God should have been laid upon this particular people. But the "scandal of particularity," as it has been called, is inseparable from an historical revelation. History consists of events. An event happens *here* and not there, *now* and not then, to *this* person (or group) and not to that. And so the revelation of God in history came to one people and not to others, with the intention that through that people it should extend ultimately to all mankind. We cannot explain this particularity.[10]

But even as events in secular history consist of occurrence plus meaning, the same is true of events in *Heilsgeschichte*.[11] Historical events in *Heilsgeschichte* consist of meaning and occurrence, and "according to the unanimous view of the biblical writers" the meaning of events in *Heilsgeschichte* "resides in a meeting of man with God."[12] At crucial points in sacred history it is "clear that a factor beyond the natural is impinging upon the natural factors and directing their outcome."[13] Thus the meaning of events in *Heilsgeschichte* is to be found in the confrontation of man with God.

Dodd's argument in this regard, that events in *Heilsgeschichte* are composed of occurrence plus meaning and that the meaning resides in a meeting of man with God, can be illustrated by the Exodus. In regard to bare *occurrence*, a group of Hebrew-speaking clans, having rebelled against Egyptian overlords, took up a nomadic life in the Sinai peninsula where they accepted the rudiments of a religious system and developed a political

---

[9]Dodd, *The Bible Today*, 125.

[10]Ibid., 107.

[11]Ibid., 99.

[12]Ibid.

[13]Ibid., 100.

consciousness. Disciplined by the Sinai experiences, they invaded Palestine and carved out territories for themselves. But these Exodus occurrences also had *meaning*. The meaning is to be found in the confrontation of Israel with God, for God was active in the Exodus experiences to accomplish his purpose. Through the Exodus, Yahweh was fashioning and molding the Jewish nation for the unique role it was to play in world history. Only when attention is given to both *occurrence* and *meaning* can the *historical event* of the Exodus be properly understood.

Thus, by way of summary, the following points are salient for understanding Dodd's philosophy of history.

1. God has revealed Himself primarily through *Heilsgeschichte,* which finds expression in the history of the Jewish people.
2. Historical events are composed of occurrence plus meaning.
3. The meaning of different historical events varies in intensity.
4. The meaning of events in *Heilsgeschichte* resides in a meeting of man with God.

2. Dodd's Philosophy of History in Relation to the Christ Event

The preceding excursus on Dodd's philosophy of history was necessary in order to provide a frame of reference from which to understand how he can speak of Jesus' ministry as realized eschatology or as the entrance of the *eschaton* into history. To grasp his thought it is important to remember that for Professor Dodd a *historical event* is *occurrence* plus *meaning* and that the intensity of meaning resident in historical events varies. Because of this variation in intensity, Dodd argued that "there may be an event which is *uniquely significant,* and this event may give a unique character to the whole series to which it belongs."[14] For Dodd, the ministry of Jesus was such an event. In the *Heilsgeschichte* process, Jesus' life, death, and resurrection was a complex in which resided a "unique intensity of significance."[15] This evaluation of Jesus' career was expressed by Professor Dodd in *History and the Gospel*.

> If now we accept the definition of history as consisting of events which are of the nature of occurrence plus meaning, we may describe the story

---

[14]Dodd, *History and the Gospel,* 29.

[15]Ibid.

of the Gospels as a narrative of events whose *meaning is eschatological,* that is to say, events in which is to be discerned the mighty act of the transcendent God which brings history to its fulfillment. There is, then, an historical and supra-historical aspect of the Gospel story. On the one hand it reveals what the saving purpose of God is eternally, in relation to all men everywhere, overruling all limitations of time and space. In this sense the Gospel is timeless, and can be preached everywhere as the present power of God unto salvation. On the other hand, it narrates the singular, unrepeatable events in which the saving purpose of God entered history at a particular moment, and altered its character.[16]

In part the preceding quotation asserts that "we may describe the story of the Gospels as a narrative of events whose *meaning is eschatological.*" This statement can be understood only if we bear in mind Dodd's concept of a historical event as meaning plus occurrence. When Dodd describes Jesus' ministry as the eschaton's entrance into history or as realized eschatology, the terms eschaton and eschatology do not have temporal connotations; rather, they are used with reference to the "meaning" of the Christ episode. Thus Dodd wrote in regard to Jesus' career,

History, indeed, still goes on, and at long last will have an ending. But meanwhile, the true *eschaton,* the event in which its meaning is conclusively revealed, has become an object of experience.[17]

Or in *The Apostolic Preaching and Its Developments,* Professor Dodd declared that the expected *eschaton* had entered history in Jesus' life.

In the *eschaton* is concentrated the whole *meaning* which, if history were to go on, might be diffused throughout a long process.[18] . . . For history depends for its *meaning* and reality upon that which is other than history. The real, inward, and eternal meaning, striving for expression in the course of history, is completely expressed in the *eschaton.*[19] . . . For the

---

[16]Ibid., 35-36; italics added.

[17]C. H. Dodd, *The Kingdom of God and History* (London: George Allen and Unwin, 1938) 24.

[18]Dodd, *The Apostolic Preaching and Its Developments,* 82; italicization of *meaning* not in the original.

[19]Ibid., 83; italicization of *meaning* not in the original.

New Testament writers in general, the *eschaton* has entered history.²⁰ . . . *The Gospel of primitive Christianity is a Gospel of realized eschatology.*²¹

There is no need for multiple examples. These quotations reveal how Professor Dodd used derivatives of *eschatos* to refer to the meaning resident in the Christ episode. To be sure, Dodd's arguments are not easy to follow, and he admitted that realized eschatology was not a felicitous term.²² But the sympathetic reader can see that Dodd was searching for words through which to express his conviction that something of infinite worth has been accomplished for man by God in Christ. Repeatedly in his writings Professor Dodd emphasized his belief that in the Christ event has occurred a divine revelation of infinite value.²³

Moreover, Professor Dodd contended that the early Church indicated the unique intensity of significance that characterized the Christ event by citing Old Testament prophecies. Thus in *History and the Gospel* Dodd wrote,

> The early Church took over a large corpus of eschatological predictions from the Old Testament and the apocalyptic literature; and from a very early period its mind was bent upon showing how these predictions were fulfilled in the story of Jesus. The study of testimony books has led to the conclusion that the application of prophecy was probably the earliest form of Christian theological thought. To our minds the methods of application often seem arbitrary and far-fetched, but the intention is clear—to show that in the life, death and resurrection of Jesus the *eschaton,* or ultimate issue of history, was indeed realized.²⁴

---

²⁰Ibid., 85.

²¹Ibid; italics added.

²²C. H. Dodd, *The Interpretation of the Fourth Gospel* (Cambridge: Cambridge University Press, 1953) 447.

²³C. H. Dodd, *The Coming of Christ* (Cambridge: Cambridge University Press, 1954) 25; *Gospel and Law* (Cambridge: Cambridge University Press, 1951) 58; *The Apostolic Preaching and Its Developments,* 33, 77, 87; *The Bible Today,* 109.

²⁴Dodd, *History and the Gospel,* 60.

This understanding of Old Testament citation was worked out in detail by Professor Dodd in *According to the Scriptures*.[25] The thesis of this book is that by employing Old Testament citations, for example, Psalm 2:7, Psalm 110:1, and Isaiah 6:9-10, early Christian writers indicated the intense significance they attached to Jesus' career.

III. An Evaluation

On first encounter I was favorably impressed with Professor Dodd's Christological version of realized eschatology as presented in works such as *History and the Gospel* and *The Apostolic Preaching and Its Developments*. I remained impressed until I encountered T. A. Roberts's *History and Christian Apologetic*, an important and neglected book.[26] Roberts broached objections to Dodd's line of reasoning. The objections Roberts raised, I suggest, may be labeled (1) an objection having to do with the *subjectivity of meaning* and (2) an objection having to do with *multiple meanings*. These objections are potent, and attention will now be given to them.

1. Subjectivity of Meaning Objection

Repeatedly Professor Dodd used the formula: *occurrence plus meaning equals historical event*. "We might indeed say that an historical 'event' is an occurrence *plus* the interest and meaning which the occurrence possessed for the persons involved in it, and by which the record is determined."[27] For Professor Dodd, a historical event is comparable to a two-sided coin; one side is the occurrence ("that which happened"), while the other side is the meaning the occurrence possessed. To express the matter another way, Professor Dodd considered meaning an element constitutive of a historical event.

This conception of historical event suggests R. G. Collingwood's distinction between the inside and the outside of an event. Professor Collingwood, British historian, wrote in his posthumously published *The Idea of History:*

---

[25] C. H. Dodd, *According to the Scriptures* (New York: Charles Scribner's Sons, 1953) 12, 13, 16, 27.

[26] T. A. Roberts, *History and Christian Apologetic* (London: S.P.C.K., 1960).

[27] Dodd, *History and the Gospel*, 27.

> The historian, investigating any event in the past, makes a distinction between what may be called the outside and the inside of an event. By the outside of the event I mean everything belonging to it which can be described in terms of bodies and their movements: the passage of Caesar, accompanied by certain men, across a river called the Rubicon at one date, or the spilling of his blood on the floor of the senate-house at another. By the inside of the event I mean that in it which can only be described in terms of thought: Caesar's defiance of Republican law, or the clash of constitutional policy between himself and his assassins. The historian is never concerned with either of these to the exclusion of the other. He is investigating not mere events (where by a mere event I mean one which has only an outside and no inside) but actions, and an action is the unity of the outside and inside of an event. He is interested in the crossing of the Rubicon only in its relation to Republican law, and in the spilling of Caesar's blood only in its relation to a constitutional conflict. His work may begin by discovering the outside of an event, but it can never end there; he must always remember that the event was an action, and that his main task is to think himself into this action, to discern the thought of its agent.[28]

Professor Dodd's historical methodology in *History and the Gospel* is obviously similar to R. G. Collingwood's. "The outside is for Dodd the bare occurrence and the inside is the full meaning which it bore for the people who experienced it."[29] Yet to the point is T. A. Roberts's observation (contra Dodd): *an event—in and of itself—has no meaning*. "Explanation, or if Dodd prefers to use the word 'meaning,' is not something that inheres to or in an event, like the core of an apple reached by peeling away the skin."[30] Events are not "things to which their meaning or explanations are attached as with a label"[31] Thus Roberts rejected as invalid Dodd's idea of significance (meaning) residing *in events per se*. The point of Mr. Roberts's criticism can be elucidated by appealing to Lockean categories. Professor Dodd viewed meaning as a primary quality residing in an event, not as a secondary quality residing within the experient. Yet meaning is—us-

---

[28]R. G. Collingwood, *The Idea of History* (London and New York: Oxford University Press, 1946).

[29]Roberts, *History and Christian Apologetic*, 92.

[30]Ibid., 93.

[31]Ibid.

ing Lockean terms—a secondary quality. It resides within the observer-participant, not within the event qua event. By its very nature a meaning assigned to an event is subjective, noetic, existing within the mind of the experient. This insight explains why R. G. Collingwood wrote, "By the inside of the event I mean that in it which can only be described in terms of thought."[32] Professor Dodd, contra Collingwood, curiously assumed that meaning was "located" *in an occurrence*. Consequently, he committed the fallacy of misplaced location when he wrote of a "unique intensity of significance"[33] residing *in an event*, or when he wrote, "In the world as we know it the outward and the inward, occurrence and meaning, are inseparably united in the event."[34]

2. Multiple Meanings Objection

Once the subjectivity of meaning is conceded (that is, meaning resides within the human mind, not outside the mind in events), then it becomes understandable how the same occurrence can have more than one meaning. Such is the case because multiple—even contradictory—meanings can be assigned to the same occurrences by different minds evaluating those occurrences. Professor Dodd assumed the life of Jesus had only *one* meaning—the meaning assigned to it by the Christian community. Yet this view is arbitrary, for other meanings were assigned to Jesus' life by other observers. To the Romans, Jesus was a rebel deserving execution. To hostile Jews, he was a heretic who led Israel astray. To say that only one of these meanings (that is, the meaning assigned by Christians) is right while the others are wrong is dubious reasoning. Clearly the meaning given to Jesus' life by Talmudic Jews was—at least to Talmudic Jews—the right meaning.

The insight being belabored is this: conflicting valuations of the same occurrence are possible. Professor Dodd did not recognize this insight. Moreover, Professor Dodd, placing emphasis upon early Christian evaluation of Jesus, overlooked the insight "that participants in events are too near and too much taken up in them to realize or to be able to assess their

---

[32]Collingwood, *The Idea of History*, 213.

[33]Dodd, *History and the Gospel*, 29.

[34]Ibid., 28.

full significance."[35] For example, does anyone believe Columbus and his companions recognized during their lifetimes the true significance of their fifteenth-century exploratory voyages? Most probably they did not. Similarly, did contemporaries recognize Jesus' true significance? Or is this recognition possible only to those who, centuries later, perceive the impact Jesus has made upon human history?

These objections—posed by T. A. Roberts—are cited as indication that Professor Dodd's Christological version of realized eschatology (as a Christian apologetic) is not without weaknesses. Yet it also has value, and we will deal with that in the next chapter.

---

[35]Roberts, *History and Christian Apologetic*, 90.

CHAPTER
• 6 •

Conclusion

"Realized eschatology" is an oxymoron. *Eschatology* suggests systematic reflection upon events that are to occur in the future. *Realized* suggests that which has already been accomplished. To combine these antithetical suggestions—as the phrase "realized eschatology" does—produces an ideological contradiction. Although an ideological contradiction, realized eschatology has become an established expression in Anglo-American theological circles.

This study has demonstrated that Professor Dodd used "realized eschatology" in different ways. He developed a *Kingdom version* to designate the view that the Kingdom was actualized in Jesus' ministry. He developed a *Christological version* to designate the view that the Christ event possesses ultimate significance (meaning). Many scholars, unaware two versions of realized eschatology exist, have found the expression to be perplexing. Thus A. W. Argyle could write an article entitled "Does 'Realized Eschatology' Make Sense?" Reflecting the confusion that surrounds any using of "realized eschatology," Argyle asserted that

> Of recent years there has come into theological literature a new phrase which is rapidly becoming an accepted "technical term." It is found not only in the writings of Professor C. H. Dodd, who apparently invented it, but in other authoritative books as well. It is used by Professor A. M. Hunter in *The Work and Words of Jesus,* and by Dr. Vincent Taylor in his commentary on St. Mark's Gospel. It seems worthwhile, therefore, to consider what the phrase means, or, indeed, whether it has any meaning at all.
>
> The word *eschatology* means the doctrine of the "last thing" (*eschaton*) or "last things" (*eschata*). The last things of what? In terms of

the New Testament, the last things "of this present evil age"; or, to use Professor Dodd's definition: "the end of history" (*The Apostolic Preaching and Its Development,* p. 207). Now "the end of history" is a conception beyond the reach or grasp of the human intellect, but it is difficult to see how the end of history could have been "realized" while history still goes on. It is therefore puzzling to read: "for the New Testament writers in general, the *eschaton* has entered into history" (C. H. Dodd, [*Apostolic Preaching*], p. 210). How could the writers of the apostolic age have believed that the "last thing" or "the end" of history had come already when history was still continuing?

Yet this is the doctrine of "realized eschatology" which is so dominant in the modern interpretation of Christian theology. According to this teaching, the Ministry, Death, and Resurrection constitute the *eschaton,* "The last thing" of history, which has broken into the midst of history. "The Gospel of primitive Christianity is a Gospel of realized eschatology" ([*Apostolic Preaching*], p. 210). This means that early Christians taught that the end of history had entered into history *before* the end of history; for, though many of them seem to have expected that this present world-order would end soon, this expectation would be incompatible with the belief that it had already come to an end. If Professor Dodd is right, therefore, it follows that the Gospel of primitive Christianity was self-contradictory.[1]

The perplexity expressed in the preceding quotation was not due to Argyle's lack of acumen; rather, his perplexity was caused by the oxymoronic nature of the phrase "realized eschatology," by the coexistence of two versions of realized eschatology (versions that are fused in the minds of most Anglo-American New Testament scholars), and by Dodd's curious failure to use terms with consistency.

Completely lacking in either biblical or patristic support, stumbling as a Christian apologetic, the Kingdom version of realized eschatology confuses rather than clarifies. The discontinuance of the Kingdom version of realized eschatology would be a positive development in Anglo-American theological circles. The probability of its discontinuance, however, is slight.

---

[1]A. W. Argyle, "Does Realized Eschatology Make Sense?" *Hibbert Journal* 51 (July 1953): 385-87, quotation from 385. In his article, Argyle cites the appendix to Dodd's *The Apostolic Preaching and Its Developments* as it first appeared in the *Transactions* of the Oxford Society of Historical Theology, that is, as pp. 207 and 210bis. The text he cites appears on pp. 84 and 85 in *The Apostolic Preaching* as separately published.

Conclusion • 115

For realized eschatology, once a hypothesis, is now a dogma, thus confirming the late Henry Cadbury's contention that a common foible in biblical studies is the transforming of hypotheses into dogmas.[2] This transforming, Professor Cadbury argued, occurs even though evidence upon which a hypothesis is based subsequently falls into disarray. The dogma of realized eschatology (the Kingdom version) is cherished by Christian apologists because it can be used to attenuate difficulties posed by consistent eschatology. It is an ideological shovel with which Christian apologists keep Johannes Weiss and Albert Schweitzer in their graves. In other words, realized eschatology is a scholarly means for engaging in intellectual dishonesty.

In the twenty-first century scholars will doubtless write books surveying New Testament studies during the twentieth century. Paragraphs in these books will be devoted to realized eschatology. In these paragraphs the Kingdom version of realized eschatology will be described as a theory that contended that "the common idea underlying all uses of the term 'the Kingdom of God' is that of the manifest and effective assertion of the divine sovereignty against all the evil of the world."[3] Scholars in the twenty-first century will also—in all likelihood—view this Kingdom version of realized eschatology as a puzzling mutation. They will ask, "In light of the insight that World War II, Auschwitz, and Buchenwald were impending, how could Professor Dodd have confidently asserted in the mid-1930s that the 'divine sovereignty' was now being effectively asserted against all the evil of the world?" In decades to come, I suggest, the Kingdom version of realized eschatology will be viewed as an optimistic theory conceived on an English university campus during the peaceful interlude between the First and Second World Wars, a theory reflecting the worldview of a well-intentioned English intellectual who failed to perceive that moral evil is still an intractable, tragic factor in human experience.

Professor Dodd's *Christological version* of realized eschatology, by contrast, has value. But this Christological version, I believe, needs modification. Walking in the footsteps of English historians like R. G. Col-

---

[2]I heard Dr. Henry Cadbury make this remark in an address delivered at the Harvard Divinity School during the 1959-1960 academic year. Professor Cadbury's protest is found in "Some Foibles of New Testament Scholarship," *The Journal of Bible and Religion* 26 (July 1958): 213-16.

[3]C. H. Dodd, *The Parables of the Kingdom* (London: James Nisbet, 1935) 50.

lingwood, influenced by the *Heilsgeschichte* movement in German theology, Professor Dodd made much of the formula: a historical event consists of occurrence plus meaning. In using this formula Professor Dodd was attempting to translate the Christian faith into modern thought forms. For this attempt we may be grateful. But this attempt does not work. In explicating why it does not work I want to elaborate further an insight I touched upon in the previous chapter, that is, that Professor Dodd fell victim to the fallacy of misplaced location. He contended that meaning resides *in an event*. But events per se do not have meaning. An event happens, and people who witness the event fabricate *within themselves* what they *perceive* to be the event's *meaning*. The intuiting of meaning (like the intuiting of beauty) is an activity of the human mind. Meaning is not an ingredient *in* an event (comparable to salt or to flour which are ingredients *in* a recipe). Rather, meaning is read into an event by people who experience the event. Moreover, different people read different meanings into the same event.

What I am contending, I trust, may be clarified through the following illustration. I teach at a state university that has a football season every fall. From September through December a series of football games are played. These games are events. They happen. On a playing field opposing teams contest one another while spectators watch. Yet these football games as events do not have meaning *in and of themselves*. Rather, different people read into these games meanings that make sense to them. A football player reasons: "For me the significance of a football game is providing an opportunity for me to display my athletic abilities. By demonstrating my skills I will possibly garner a professional football contract." An alumnus reasons: "For me the significance of a football game is providing an occasion to return to campus and to visit with classmates I haven't seen for years." The manager of the local McDonald's, located two blocks off campus, reasons: "For me the significance of a football game is a dramatic increase in hamburger sales. A football game means extra profit." The event for the football player, the alumnus, and the McDonald's manager is the same: A football game played on a pleasant Saturday afternoon. Yet they derive from this same event different meanings. These diverse meanings reside within the football player, the alumnus, and the McDonald's manager—not within the event per se. Thus Professor Dodd's formula (event equals occurrence plus its inherent meaning) is not convincing.

The Christological version of realized eschatology could be made more convincing, I suggest, if the concept of *person* was utilized instead of the concept of *event*. The *eschaton* (that which is ultimate in religious significance) has been realized in a *person*. Realized eschatology, so modified, would designate the theological view that at the heart of the Christian faith is a Person and a Life, not a dogmatic system or an ethical code. St. Paul was aware of this insight when he wrote to the Corinthian Christians, "It was the god who said 'Let light shine out of darkness' who has shone in our hearts to give unto us the light of the knowledge of the glory of God *in the face of Christ Jesus.*" This insight was driven home to me years ago in a sermon I heard preached in Cambridge, Massachusetts. During the late 1950s I was a student for a year at the Harvard Divinity School. The pastor of the Old Cambridge Baptist Church at the time was Dr. Samuel Miller, who later became dean of Harvard Divinity School. Sunday after Sunday I attended the Old Cambridge Baptist Church to worship and to hear Dr. Miller's thought-provoking sermons. One February Sunday the weather was miserably cold, and I was tempted not to attend services. Enduring a New England snow storm, I went to church anyway. I have always been grateful I attended because Dr. Miller preached a sermon that Sunday I have never forgotten. The sermon was entitled "God Spoke to Us in a Person." In his discourse Dr. Miller contended that you and I are most profoundly influenced in life by persons—our parents, our teachers, our peers. The genius of the Christian faith, Dr. Miller argued, is that when God decided to reveal Himself he did so in a *person*—Jesus of Nazareth. In Jesus' life and personality we—as Christians—have been given a problematical glimpse of who God is and what he is like. At the heart of Judaism is Torah. At the heart of Islam is the Koran and the Five Pillars. At the heart of Buddhism is a belief complex—the Four Noble Truths and the Eightfold Path. But at the heart of the Christian religion is a person who across the centuries has exerted an influence upon millions of people from all walks of life.

These millions view Jesus as a charismatic person who has significance for them. But a question that must be confronted is: "How does Jesus come to have significance—or meaning—for the Christian believer?" Through what process does the Christian believer interiorize a sense of meaning so that he asserts, "Jesus has meaning *for me* in the sense that I recognize in him the One through whom God has spoken to mankind." An awakening within us of a conviction of Jesus' significance is, I believe, not something we accomplish by ourselves. Rather (to use Pauline language) "the Spirit of God joins with our spirit"—encouraging and enabling us to recognize Jesus as lord of life. To our modern ears this biblical language sounds curious. Yet this biblical language can be translated into contemporary thought concepts. Ernst Troeltsch, German theologian of the first part of this century, dealt extensively with how religion functions within man's mental structure. Following Kant, Troeltsch posited the existence within man's mental structure of a religious a priori (in addition to a theoretical, a moral, and an aesthetic a priori). This religious a priori—and here I am following Paul Tillich—is the point within man's mental structure where the Infinite and the finite (God and man) meet. This religious a priori has its own kind of certainty. Through this religious a priori, God stimulates and encourages within the believer this conviction: Jesus is Lord of life.

The problem is, Christians want to refashion this Jesus into a person of their preferences. They prefer a Jesus who never made a mistake and who was thousands of years ahead of his time. They prefer a Jesus who resembles a confident Methodist bishop, an eminent Presbyterian divine, or a First-Baptist-Church parson who quotes Shakespeare. But this is not the Jesus we encounter in the Gospels. The Jesus we confront in the Gospels performed healings, expounded the Torah, debated his opponents, and antagonized both the Romans and the Jewish religious aristocracy—an antagonizing that led to his crucifixion. He also proclaimed the imminent arrival on earth of the Kingdom of God—a Golden Age for Jews. This proclamation turned out to be an error. This error (which has troubled sensitive Christians across the centuries) suggests that Jesus—like all people—experienced historical relativism. Troubled, inquisitive Christians overlook this insight: there is no a priori reason why the Jesus who experienced historical relativism could not have been transformed by the power of God into the Risen Lord of Christian devotion—the One who lives in the *kerygma* and worship of the Church. Inquisitive Christians also overlook the insight that God's resurrecting of Jesus, mistaken proclaimer of the Kingdom of God, carries a comforting implication: *belief accuracy or doctrinal rectitude is not a prerequisite for divine approval.* The Christological version of realized eschatology is, I conclude, a possible new wineskin within which the Christian message can be conveyed to reflective people in our time.

APPENDIX
• I •

A Listing of All References to Kingdom in the Synoptic Gospels

1. Logia That Either Emphasize the Nearness of the Kingdom or Present the Kingdom as a Future Hope

Matthew 3:1-2 In those days came John the Baptist, preaching in the wilderness of Judea, "Repent, for the *kingdom of heaven* is at hand."

Matthew 4:17 From that time Jesus began to preach, saying, "Repent, for the *kingdom of heaven* is at hand."

Matthew 6:10a "Thy *kingdom* come."

Matthew 10:7 And preach as you go, saying, "The *kingdom of heaven* is at hand."

Matthew 12:28 "But if it is by the Spirit of God that I cast out demons, then the *kingdom of God* has come upon you."

Matthew 16:28 "Truly, I say to you, there are some standing here who will not taste death before they see the Son of man coming in his *kingdom*."

Matthew 25:34 Then the King will say to those at his right hand, "Come, O blessed of my Father, inherit the *kingdom* prepared for you from the foundation of the world."

Mark 1:14-15 Now after John was arrested, Jesus came into Galilee, preaching the gospel of God, and saying, "The time is fulfilled, and the *Kingdom of God* is at hand; repent, and believe in the gospel."

Mark 9:1 And he said to them, "Truly, I say to you, there are some standing here who will not taste death before they see the *kingdom of God* come with power."

Mark 11:10 "Blessed be the *kingdom* of our father David that is coming! Hosanna in the highest!"

Mark 15:43 Joseph of Arimathea, a respected member of the council, who was also himself looking for the *kingdom of God,* took courage and went to Pilate, and asked for the body of Jesus.

Luke 9:27 "But I tell you truly, there are some standing here who will not taste of death before they see the *kingdom of God.*"

Luke 10:9 "Heal the sick in it and say to them, 'The *kingdom of God* has come near you.' "

Luke 10:11 "Even the dust of your own town that clings to our feet, we wipe off against you; nevertheless know this, that the *kingdom of God* has come near."

Luke 11:2 And he said to them "When you pray, say: Father, hallowed be thy name. Thy *kingdom* come."

Luke 11:20 "But if it is by the finger of God that I cast out demons, then the *kingdom of God* has come upon you."

Luke 19:11 As they heard these things, he proceeded to tell a parable, because he was near to Jerusalem, and because they supposed that the *kingdom of God* was to appear immediately.

Luke 21:31 "So also when you see these things taking place, you know that the *kingdom of God* is near."

Luke 23:42 And he said, "Jesus, remember me when you come in your *kingdom.*"

Luke 23:50-51 Now there was a man named Joseph from the Jewish town of Arimathea. He was a member of the council, a good and righteous man, who had not consented to their purpose and deed, and he was looking for the *kingdom of God.*

2. Logia Dealing with Eating, Drinking, and Sitting in the Kingdom

Matthew 8:11-12 "I tell you, many will come from east and west and sit at table with Abraham, Isaac, and Jacob in the *kingdom of heaven,* while the sons of the kingdom will be thrown into the outer darkness, there men will weep and gnash their teeth."

Matthew 26:29 "I tell you I shall not drink again of this fruit of the vine until that day when I drink it new with you in my Father's *kingdom.*"

Mark 14:25 "Truly, I say to you, I shall not drink again of the fruit of the vine until that day when I drink it new in the *kingdom of God.*"

Luke 13:29 "And many will come from east and west, and from north and south, and sit at table in the *kingdom of God.*"

Luke 14:15 When one of those who sat at table with him heard this, he said to him, "Blessed is he who shall eat bread in the *kingdom of God.*"

Luke 22:15-18 And he said to them, "I have earnestly desired to eat this passover with you before I suffer; for I tell you I shall not eat it until it is fulfilled in the *kingdom of God.*" And he took a cup, and when he had given thanks he said, "Take this, and divide it among yourselves; for I tell you that from now on I shall not drink of the fruit of the vine until the *kingdom of God* comes."

Luke 22:28-30 "You are those who have continued with me in my trials; as my Father appointed a *kingdom* for me, so do I appoint for you that you may eat and drink at my table in my *kingdom,* and sit on thrones judging the twelve tribes of Israel."

3. Logia Presenting the Kingdom as an Object of Vision

Matthew 16:28 "Truly I say to you, there are some standing here who will not taste death before they see the Son of man coming in his *kingdom.*"

Mark 9:1 "Truly I say to you there are some standing here who will not taste death before they see the *kingdom of God* come with power."

Luke 9:27 "But I tell you truly, there are some standing here who will not taste of death before they see the *kingdom of God.*"

Luke 13:28 "There you will weep and gnash your teeth, when you see Abraham and Isaac and Jacob and all the prophets in the *kingdom of God* and you yourselves thrust out."

4. Logia Concerned with Status in the Kingdom

Matthew 5:19 "Whosoever then relaxes one of the least of these commandments and teaches men so, shall be called least in the *kingdom of heaven;* but he who does them and teaches them shall be called great in the *kingdom of heaven.*"

Matthew 11:11 "Truly, I say to you, among those born of women there has risen no one greater than John the Baptist; yet he who is least in the *kingdom of heaven* is greater than he."

Matthew 18:1, 4 At that time the disciples came to Jesus, saying, "Who is the greatest in the *kingdom of heaven?*" . . . "Whoever humbles himself like this child, he is the greatest in the *kingdom of heaven.*"

Matthew 20:21 And he said to her, "What do you want?" She said to him, "Command that these two sons of mine may sit, one at your right hand and one at your left in your *kingdom.*"

Luke 7:28 "I tell you, among those born of women none is greater than John; yet he who is least in the *kingdom of God* is greater than he."

Luke 22:28-30 "You are those who have continued with me in my trials; as my Father appointed a *kingdom* for me, so do I appoint for you that you may eat and drink at my table in my *kingdom,* and sit on thrones judging the twelve tribes of Israel."

5. The Entry Logia

Matthew 5:20 "For I tell you, unless your righteousness exceeds that of the scribes and Pharisees, you will never enter the *kingdom of heaven*."

Matthew 7:21 "Not every one who says to me, 'Lord, Lord,' shall enter the *kingdom of heaven*, but he who does the will of my Father who is in heaven."

Matthew 18:1-3 At that time the disciples came to Jesus, saying, "Who is the greatest in the *kingdom of heaven*?" And calling him a child, he put him in the midst of them, and said, "Truly, I say to you, unless you turn and become like children, you will never enter the *kingdom of heaven*."

Matthew 19:23-24 And Jesus said to his disciples, "Truly, I say to you, it will be hard for a rich man to enter the *kingdom of heaven*. Again, I tell you, it is easier for a camel to go through the eye of a needle than for a rich man to enter the *kingdom of heaven*."

Matthew 21:31b Jesus said to them, "Truly, I say to you, the tax collectors and the harlots go into the *kingdom of God* before you."

Matthew 23:13 "But woe to you, scribes and Pharisees, hypocrits! because you shut the *kingdom of heaven* against men; for you neither enter yourselves, nor allow those who would enter to go in."

Mark 9:47 "And if your eye causes you to sin, pluck it out; it is better for you to enter the *kingdom of God* with one eye than with two eyes to be thrown into hell."

Mark 10:23-25 And Jesus looked around and said to his disciples, "How hard it will be for those who have riches to enter the *kingdom of God!*" And the disciples were amazed at his word. But Jesus said to them again, "Children, how hard it is to enter the *kingdom of God!* it is easier for a camel to go through the eye of a needle than for a rich man to enter the *kingdom of God*."

Luke 18:17 "Truly, I say to you, whoever does not receive the *kingdom of God* like a child shall not enter it."

Luke 18:24-25 Jesus looking at him said, "How hard it is for those who have riches to enter the *kingdom of God!* For it is easier for a camel to go through the eye of a needle than for a rich man to enter the *kingdom of God*."

6. The Kingdom as the Object of a Proclamation

Matthew 4:23 And he went about all Galilee, teaching in their synagogues and preaching the gospel of the *kingdom* and healing every disease and every infirmity among the people.

Matthew 9:35 And Jesus went about all the cities and villages, teaching in their synagogues and preaching the gospel of the *kingdom*, and healing every disease and every infirmity.

Matthew 24:14 "And this gospel of the *kingdom* will be preached throughout the whole world, as a testimony to all nations; and then the end will come."

Luke 4:43 But he said to them, "I must preach the good news of the *kingdom of God* to the other cities also; for I was sent for this purpose."

Luke 8:1 Soon afterward he went on through cities and villages, preaching and bringing the good news of the *kingdom of God.*

Luke 9:1-2 And he called the twelve together and gave them power and authority over all demons and to cure diseases, and he sent them out to preach the *kingdom of God* and to heal.

Luke 9:11b He welcomed them and spoke to them of the *kingdom of God,* and cured those who had need of healing.

Luke 9:60 But he said to him, "Leave the dead to bury their own dead; but as for you, go and proclaim the *kingdom of God.*"

Luke 16:16 "The law and the prophets were until John; since then the good news of the *kingdom of God* is preached."

7. The Parables of the Kingdom

Matthew 13:19 "When anyone hears the word of the *kingdom* and does not understand it, the evil one comes and snatches away what is sown in his heart."

Matthew 13:24 Another parable he put before them, saying, "The *kingdom of heaven* may be compared to a man who sowed good seed in his field."

Matthew 13:31 Another parable he put before them, saying, "The *kingdom of heaven* is like a grain of mustard seed which a man took and sowed in his field."

Matthew 13:33 He told them another parable. "The *kingdom of heaven* is like leaven which a woman took and hid in three measures of meal, till it was all leavened."

Matthew 13:38a "The field is the world, and the good seed means the sons of the *kingdom.*"

Matthew 13:41 "The Son of man will send his angels, and they will gather out of his *kingdom* all causes of sin and all evildoers."

Matthew 13:43a "Then the righteous will shine like the sun in the *kingdom* of their Father."

Matthew 13:44a "The *kingdom of heaven* is like treasure hidden in a field, which a man found and covered up."

Matthew 13:45 "Again, the *kingdom of heaven* is like a merchant in search of fine pearls."

Matthew 13:47 "Again, the *kingdom of heaven* is like a net which was thrown into the sea and gathered fish of every kind."

Matthew 18:23 "Therefore the *kingdom of heaven* may be compared to a king who wished to settle accounts with his servants."

Matthew 20:1 "For the *kingdom of heaven* is like a householder who went out early in the morning to hire laborers for his vineyard."

Matthew 22:2 "The *kingdom of heaven* may be compared to a king who gave a marriage feast for his son."

Matthew 25:1 "Then the *kingdom of heaven* shall be compared to ten maidens who took their lamps and went out to meet the bridegroom."

Mark 4:26 And he said, "The *kingdom of God* is as if a man should scatter seed upon the ground."

Mark 4:30-31a And he said, "With what can we compare the *kingdom of God*, or what parable shall we use for it? It is like a grain of mustard seed."

Luke 13:18-19a He said therefore, "What is the *kingdom* of God like? And to what shall I compare it? It is like a grain of mustard seed which a man took and sowed in his garden."

Luke 13:20-21 And again he said, "to what shall I compare the *kingdom of God?* It is like leaven which a woman took and hid in three measures of meal, till it was all leavened."

8. Miscellaneous Passages

Matthew 5:3 "Blessed are the poor in spirit, for theirs is the *kingdom of heaven.*"

Matthew 5:10 "Blessed are those who are persecuted for righteousness sake, for theirs is the *kingdom of heaven.*"

Matthew 6:33 "But seek first his *kingdom* and his righteousness, and all these things shall be yours as well."

Matthew 11:12 "From the days of John the Baptist until now the *kingdom of heaven* has suffered violence, and men of violence take it by force."

Matthew 13:11 And he answered them, "To you it has been given to know the secrets of the *kingdom of heaven,* but to them it has not been given."

Matthew 13:52 And he said to them, "Therefore every scribe who has been trained for the *kingdom of heaven* is like a householder who brings out of his treasure what is new and what is old."

Matthew 16:19a "I will give you the eyes of the *kingdom of heaven.*"

Matthew 19:12b "There are eunuchs who have made themselves eunuchs for the sake of the *kingdom of heaven*. He who is able to receive this, let him receive it."

Matthew 19:14 Jesus said, "Let the children come to me, and do not hinder them; for to such belongs the *kingdom of heaven.*"

Matthew 21:43 "Therefore I tell you, the *kingdom of God* will be taken away from you and given to a nation producing the fruits of it."

Mark 4:11 And he said to them, "To you has been given the secret of the *kingdom of God,* but for those outside everything is in parables."

Mark 10:14-15 But when Jesus saw it he was indignant, and said to them, "Let the children come to me, do not hinder them; for to such belongs the *kingdom of God.* Truly, I say to you, whoever does not receive the *kingdom of God* like a child shall not enter it."

Mark 12:34 And when Jesus saw that he answered wisely, he said to him, "You are not far from the *kingdom of God."*

Luke 6:20b "Blessed are you poor, for yours is the *kingdom of heaven."*

Luke 8:10a "To you it has been given to know the secrets of the *kingdom of God."*

Luke 9:62 Jesus said to him, "No one who puts his hand to the plow and looks back is fit for the *kingdom of God."*

Luke 12:31 "Instead, seek his *kingdom,* and these things shall be yours as well."

Luke 12:32 "Fear not, little flock, for it is your Father's good pleasure to give you the *kingdom."*

Luke 17:20-21 Being asked by the Pharisees when the *kingdom of God* was coming, he answered them, "The *kingdom of God* is not coming with signs to be observed; nor will they say, 'Lo, here it is!' or "There!' for behold, the *kingdom of God* is in the midst of you."

Luke 18:16 "But Jesus called them to him, saying! "Let the children come to me, and do not hinder them; for to such belongs the *kingdom of God."*

Luke 18:29-30 And he said to them, "Truly, I say to you, there is no man who has left house or wife or brothers or parents or children, for the sake of the *kingdom of God,* who will not receive manifold more in this time, and in the age to come, eternal life."

9. Logia That Refer to a Kingdom, But Not to the Kingdom of God

Matthew 4:8 Again, the devil took him to a very high mountain, and showed him all the *kingdoms* of the world and the glory of them.

Matthew 12:25-26 Knowing their thoughts, he said to them, "Every *kingdom* divided against itself is laid waste, and no city or house divided against itself will stand; and if Satan casts out Satan, he is divided against himself; how then will his *kingdom* stand?"

Matthew 24:7a "For nation will rise against nation, and *kingdom* against *kingdom."*

Mark 3:24 "If a *kingdom* is divided against itself, that *kingdom* cannot stand."

Mark 6:23 And he vowed to her, "Whatever you ask me, I will give you, even half of my *kingdom."*

Mark 13:8a "For nation will rise against nation, and *kingdom* against *kingdom."*

Luke 4:5 And the devil took him up, and showed him all the *kingdoms* of the world in a moment of time.

Luke 11:17-18a But he, knowing their thought, said to them, "Every *kingdom* divided against itself is laid waste, and house falls upon house. And if Satan is also divided against himself, how will his *kingdom* stand?"

Luke 19:12 He said therefore, "A nobleman went into a far country to receive a *kingdom* and then return."

Luke 19:15a When he returned, having received the *kingdom,* he commanded these servants, to whom he had given the money, to be called.

Luke 21:10 Then he said to them, "Nation will rise against nation, and *kingdom* against *kingdom.*"

APPENDIX
• II •

The Kingdom of God in Patristic Literature

There is reason to assume continuity between Jesus' proclamation of the *basileia* and the understanding of *basileia* in patristic thought. That Jesus' teaching on this issue was transmitted by oral and written means from the first generation of disciples to succeeding generations is probable. Yet many attempts to understand the Kingdom of God have ignored evidence in the early Church Fathers.[1] Because of proximity to the original tradition, evidence from patristic literature is relevant to any discussion of the *basileia*.

In doing research for this book I read what I judged to be the most important patristic literature through Eusebius of Caesarea. A study of these

---

[1] Outside the Synoptics there are few references in the New Testament to the Kingdom of God. This paucity is probably to be explained by the ad hoc nature of much New Testament material. It is easy to understand, for example, why there is no prolonged explication of the *basileia* in a letter like Galatians, which was written specifically to deal with the Judaistic controversy. Verses wherein "kingdom" or "kingdom of God" or "kingdom of Christ" or "kingdom of his beloved Son" occur are John 3:3, 5; 18:36; Acts 1:3, 6; 8:12; 14:22; 19:8; 20:25; 28:23, 31; Romans 14:17; 1 Corinthians 4:20; 6:9-10; 15:24, 50; Galatians 5:21; Ephesians 5:5; Colossians 1:13, 4:11; 1 Thessalonians 2:12; 2 Thessalonians 1:5; 2 Timothy 4:1, 18; Hebrews 1:8; 11:33; 12:28; James 2:5; 2 Peter 1:11; Revelation 1:6, 9; 5:10; 11:15; 12:10; 17:12, 17, 18. Because in these verses the Kingdom is not dealt with extensively, it is impossible to use such references to reach a meaningful understanding of the *basileia*. However, as A. E. J. Rawlinson has pointed out in "The Kingdom of God in the Apostolic Age," *Theology* 14 (May 1927): 262-66, in the epistolary literature of the New Testament, the Kingdom is thought of as a hope for the future. "How essentially 'eschatological' and 'supernatural' is the Pauline conception of the kingdom is made evident by the brusque statement that 'flesh and blood' (i.e., human nature in its present condition) cannot inherit the kingdom of God." (264)

writings substantiates the view that the Kingdom was originally conceived as a place. Moreover, a study of patristic literature reveals that for the postapostolic Church the Kingdom was a *future hope*. There is no suggestion that the Kingdom was considered (as Dodd suggested) a "pure reality which we partly apprehend in the most exalted moments of our human experience in time."[2]

In patristic literature, the devotees of realized eschatology are confronted with data antithetical to their abstract understanding of the Kingdom of God. This data raises unavoidable questions. If Jesus taught the Kingdom was an abstract curative power operative in his person, why did the apostolic and postapostolic Church misunderstand him and conceive of the Kingdom in spatial terms? Moreover, if Jesus conceived of the Kingdom as a present reality, why did the apostolic and postapostolic Church misunderstand him and conceive of the Kingdom as a future hope?

1. The Evidence of the Apostolic Fathers

References to the Kingdom in the Apostolic Fathers are not numerous.[3] Nonetheless, the references that do occur portray the Kingdom as a future hope.

a. I Clement

Penned toward the close of Diocletian's persecution, this epistle was written in the name of the Roman Church to the Christian brotherhood in Corinth. Clement, bishop of the Roman Christians, wrote the following regarding the *basileia:*

> The Apostles received the Gospel for us from the Lord Jesus Christ; Jesus Christ was sent forth from God. So then Christ is from God, and the Apostles are from Christ. Both therefore came of the will of God in the appointed order. Having therefore received a charge, and having been fully assured through the resurrection of our Lord Jesus Christ and con-

---

[2]C. H. Dodd, *The Apostolic Preaching and Its Developments* (London: Hodder and Stoughton, 1936; New York: Harper and Row, ᵖᵗ1964, 1937) 84.

[3]In studying the Apostolic Fathers I used the following: J. B. Lightfoot, *The Apostolic Fathers* vol. 2 (Cambridge: Harvard University Press, 1913). Limitation of space precludes the citing of all the evidence. The *basileia* is conceived as a future hope in *The Epistle to Diognetus* 10.2; *The Shepherd of Hermas* 12.3–13.2, 15.2–16.4, 20.2-3, 29.2, 31.2; *The Epistle of St. Ignatius to the Ephesians* 16.1-2.

firmed in the word of God with full assurance of the Holy Ghost, they went forth with the glad tidings that the Kingdom of God *should come.*
(1 Clement 42:1-3; italics added)

All the generations from Adam unto this day have passed away: but they that by God's grace were perfected in love dwell in the abode of the pious; and they shall be made manifest in the visitation of the Kingdom of God [οἱ φανερωθήσονται ἐν τῇ ἐπισκοπῇ τῆς βασιλείας τοῦ θεοῦ]. For it is written: Enter into the closet for a very little while, until my anger and my wrath shall pass away, and I will remember a good day and will raise you from your tombs. (1 Clement 50:2-4)

The preceding quotation collocates the coming of the Kingdom and the resurrection from the dead. The futuristic implication is obvious.

b. 2 Clement

In *2 Clement,* an ancient homily dating from about A.D. 120 to 140, the following references to the *basileia* appear.

Wherefore, brethren, let us forsake our sojourn in this world and do the will of Him that called us, and let us not be afraid to depart out of this world. For the Lord saith, "Ye shall be as lambs in the midst of wolves." But Peter answered and said unto him, "What then, if the wolves should tear the lambs?" Jesus said unto Peter, "Let not the lambs fear the wolves after they are dead; and ye also, fear ye not them that kill you and are not able to do anything to you; but fear him that after ye are dead hath power over soul and body, to cast them into the gehenna of fire. *And ye know, brethren, that the sojourn of this flesh in this world is mean and for a short time, but the promise of Christ is great and marvellous, even the rest of the Kingdom that shall be and of life eternal* [ἡ δὲ ἐπαγγελία τοῦ χριστοῦ μεγάλη καὶ θαυμαστή ἐστιν, καὶ ἀνάπαυσις τῆς μελλούσης βασιλείας καὶ ζωῆς αἐωνίου]. What then can we do to obtain them, but walk in holiness and righteousness, and consider these worldly things as alien to us, and not desire them.
(2 Clement 5:1-6; italics added)

And let not any one of you say that this flesh is not judged neither riseth again. Understand ye. In what were ye saved? In what did ye recover your sight? If ye were not in the flesh. We ought therefore to guard the flesh as a temple of God: for in like manner as ye were called in the flesh, he shall come also in the flesh. If Christ the Lord who saved us, being first spirit, then became flesh and so called us, in like manner also shall we

> in this flesh receive our reward. Let us therefore love one another, that we all may come into the Kingdom of God. (2 Clement 9:1-6)
>
> Wherefore, my brethren, let us not be double-minded but endure patiently in hope, that we may also obtain our reward. For faithful is he that promised to pay to each man the recompense of his works. If therefore we shall have wrought righteousness in the sight of God, we shall enter into his Kingdom and shall receive the promises [ἐὰν οὖν, ποιήσωμεν τὴν δικαιοσύνην ἐωαντίον τοῦ θεοῦ, εἰσήξομεν εἰς τὴν βασιλείαν αὐτοῦ καὶ ληψόμεθα τὰς ἐπαγγελίας] which ear hath not heard nor eye seen, neither hath it entered into the heart of man. (2 Clement 11:5-7)
>
> Let us therefore *await the Kingdom of God* betimes in love and righteousness, since *we know not the day* of God's appearing. For the Lord himself, being asked by a certain person when his Kingdom would come, said, "When the two shall be one, and the outside as inside, and the male with the female, neither male nor female." Now the two are one, when we speak truth among ourselves, and in two bodies there shall be one soul without dissimulation. And by "the outside as the inside" he meaneth this: by the inside he meaneth the soul and by the outside the body. Therefore in like manner as thy body appeareth, so also let the soul be manifest in its good works. And by "the male with the female, neither male or female," he meaneth this: that a brother seeing a sister should have no thought of her as a female, and that a sister seeing a brother should have no thought of him as a male. These things if he do, the Kingdom of my Father *shall come*. (2 Clement 12:1-6; italics added)

In these quotations the Kingdom is obviously a future hope.

c. The Epistle of Polycarp to the Philippians

In the epistle of Polycarp to the Philippians a reference to the Kingdom appears in the context of ethical exhortations.

> In like manner also the younger men must be blameless in all things, caring for purity before everything and curbing themselves from every evil. For it is a good thing to refrain from lusts in the world, for every lust warreth against the Spirit and neither whoremongers nor effeminate persons nor defilers of themselves with men shall inherit [κληρονομήσουσιν] the Kingdom of God, neither they that do untoward things. (Polyc. Phil. 5:3)

The closing part of the preceding quotation reflects 1 Corinthians 6:9-10; the futuristic reference to the Kingdom is obvious.

d. The Didache

The two references to the Kingdom in the *Didache* are of interest because of the distinction made between Kingdom and Church.

> But as touching the eucharistic thanksgiving give ye thanks thus. First, as regards the cup: We give Thee thanks, O our Father, for the holy vine of Thy son David, which Thou madest known unto us through Thy Son Jesus; Thine is the glory for ever and ever. As this broken bread was scattered upon the mountains and being gathered together became one, so may Thy Church be gathered together from the ends of the earth into Thy Kingdom; for Thine is the glory and the power through Jesus Christ for ever and ever. (Didache 9:1-4)

> Remember, Lord, Thy Church to deliver it from all evil and to perfect it in Thy love; and gather it together from the four winds—even the Church which has been sanctified—into Thy Kingdom which Thou hast prepared for it. (Didache 11:5)

In these *Didache* quotations the Kingdom is conceived as the goal of the Church.

e. *The Epistle of Barnabas*

The Epistle of Barnabas teaches that the Resurrection's purpose is the glorification of Christians in the Kingdom of God.

> It is good therefore to learn the ordinances of the Lord, as many as have been written above, and to walk in them. For he that doeth these things shall be glorified [ὁ γὰρ ταῦτα ποιῶν ἐν τῇ βασιλείᾳ τοῦ θεοῦ δοξασθήσεται] in the Kingdom of God; whereas he that chooseth their opposites shall perish together with his works. For this cause is the resurrection [διὰ τοῦτο ἀνάστασις], for this the recompense. I entreat those of you who are in higher station, if ye will receive any counsel of good advice from me, keep amongst you those to whom ye may do good. Fail not. The day is at hand, in which everything shall be destroyed together with the Evil One. The Lord is at hand and His reward.
> (Barnabas 21:1-3)

2. Irenaeus

Irenaeus (c. 142-200), for a number of years the Bishop of Lyons in Gaul, is primarily remembered for his anti-Gnostic treatise *Against Heresies (Adversus omnes haereses)*.[4] There are scores of places in *Against Heresies* where the Kingdom was presented as a future hope and an object of sensory perception.[5] Detailed attention, however, will be given to only one citation from this work. The citation includes Irenaeus's discussion of the predicted blessings of Genesis 27:28-29. Irenaeus referred these blessings to the future Kingdom of God. It would be difficult to conceive of the Kingdom in more concrete terms than the following:

> The predicted blessing, therefore, belongs unquestionably to the times of the kingdom, when the righteous shall bear rule upon their rising from the dead; when also the creation, having been renovated and set free, shall fructify with an abundance of all kinds of food, from the dew of heaven, and from the fertility of the earth: as the elders who saw John, the disciple of the Lord, related that they had heard from him how the Lord used to teach in regard to these times, and say: The days will come, in which vines shall grow, each having ten thousand branches, and in each branch ten thousand twigs, and in each true twig ten thousand shoots, and in each one of the shoots ten thousand clusters, and on every one of the clusters ten thousand grapes, and every grape when pressed will give five and twenty metretes of wine. And when any one of the saints shall lay hold of a cluster, another shall cry out, "I am a better cluster, take me; bless the Lord through me." In like manner [the Lord declared] that a grain of wheat would produce ten thousand ears, and that every ear should have ten thousand grains, and every grain would yield ten pounds of clear, pure, fine flour; and that all other fruit-bearing trees, and seeds and grass, would produce in similar proportions; and that all animals feeding [only] on the productions of the earth, should [in those days] become peaceful and harmonious among each other, and be in perfect subjection to man.
>
> And these things are borne witness to in writing by Papias, the hearer of John, and a companion of Polycarp, in his fourth book; for there are

---

[4]The Irenaeus quotations are from A. Cleveland Coxe, ed., *The Apostolic Fathers with Justin Matryr and Irenaeus,* vol. 1 of the American Edition of *The Ante-Nicene Fathers,* Alexander Roberts and James Donaldson, gen. eds., 10 vols. (Grand Rapids: Eerdmans, 1956 rpt. of 1885 ed.).

[5]*Against Heresies,* I.6.3, IV.20.11, IV.21.1, IV.22.2, IV.24.2, IV.27.2-4, I.28.2, IV.36.8, IV.37.7, IV.40.2, V.9.1-4, V.10.2, V.26.2.

five books compiled by him. And he says in addition, "Now these things are credible to believers." And he says that, "when the traitor Judas did not give credit to them, and put the question, 'How then can things about to bring forth so abundantly be wrought by the Lord?' the Lord declared, 'They who shall come to these [times] shall see.' " When prophesying of these times, therefore, Esaias says: "The wolf also shall feed with the lamb, and the leopard shall take his rest with the kid; the calf also, and the bull, and the lion shall eat together; and a little boy shall lead them. The ox and the bear shall feed together, and the lion shall eat straw as well as the ox. And the infant boy shall thrust his hand into the asp's den, into the nest also of the adder's brood; and they shall do no harm, nor have power to hurt anything in my holy mountain." And again he says, in recapitulation, "the lion shall eat straw like the ox, and the serpent earth as if it were bread; and they shall neither hurt nor annoy anything in my holy mountain, saith the Lord." (*Against Heresies* V.33.3-4)

Irenaeus protests all attempts to allegorize the sensory descriptions of the Kingdom in these words,

Now all these things being such as they are, cannot be understood in reference to supercelestial matters; "for God," it is said, "will show to the whole earth that is under heaven thy glory." But in the times of the kingdom, the earth has been called again by Christ to its pristine condition, and Jerusalem rebuilt after the pattern of the Jerusalem above, of which the prophet Isaiah says, "Behold, I have depicted thy walls upon my hands, and thou art always in my sight." (*Against Heresies* V.34.2)

The description of the Kingdom in the last four chapters of *Against Heresies* is far removed from Dodd's quasi-Platonic presentation.

3. Tertullian

Because he was a prolific writer and the first ecclesiastic of prominence to use Latin, Tertullian (c. 150-225) has been given the title of father of Latin theology.[6] In the writings of Tertullian, as in the writings of Irenaeus, the Kingdom was conceived as a future hope.[7] For example, in his

---

[6]The Tertullian quotations that follow are from A. Cleveland Coxe, ed., *Latin Christianity: Its Founder, Tertullian,* vol. 3 of the *Ante-Nicene Fathers,* cited above, n. 4.

[7]*On Idolatry,* ch. 9; *De Spectaculis,* ch. 30; *On Prescription Against Heretics,* ch. 13; *A Treatise on the Soul,* ch. 55; *Tertullian Against Marcion,* book 4, chs. 30 and 39.

exegesis of the Pauline statement that "flesh and blood cannot inherit the Kingdom of God" Tertullian wrote,

> How then is it, that the soul, which is the real author of the works of the flesh, shall attain to the kingdom of God, after the deeds done in the body have been atoned for, whilst the body, which was nothing but the soul's ministering agent, must remain in condemnation? Is the cup to be punished, but the poisoner to escape: Not that we indeed claim the kingdom of God for the flesh: all we do is, to assert a resurrection for the substance thereof, as the gate of the kingdom through which it is entered. But the resurrection is one thing, and the kingdom is another. *The resurrection is first, and afterwards the kingdom. We say, therefore, that the flesh rises again, but that when changed it obtains the kingdom.* "For the dead shall be raised incorruptible," even those who had been corruptible when their bodies fell into decay; "and we shall be changed, in a moment, in the twinkling of an eye. For this corruptible"—and as he spake, the apostle seemingly pointed to his own flesh—"must put on incorruption, and this mortal must put on immortality," in order, indeed, that it may be rendered a fit substance for the kingdom of God. "For we shall be like the angels." This will be the perfect change of our flesh—only after its resurrection. Now if, on the contrary, there is to be no flesh, how then shall it put on incorruption and immortality? Having then become something else by its change, it will obtain the kingdom of God, no longer the old flesh and blood, but the body which God shall have given it. Rightly then does the apostle declare, "Flesh and blood cannot inherit the kingdom of God;" for this honour does he ascribe to the changed condition which ensues on the resurrection.
>
> (*Against Marcion* 5.10)

This argument by Tertullian with reference to a transformation of the flesh reveals his concrete conception of the *basileia*. Note also the following extracts from his treatise *On the Resurrection of the Flesh*.

> Now, if even parables obscure not the light of the gospel, how unlikely it is that plain sentences and declarations, which have an unmistakable meaning, should signify any other things than their literal sense! But it is by such declarations and sentences that the Lord sets forth either the last judgment, or the kingdom, or the resurrection: "It shall be more tolerable," He says, "for Tyre and Sidon in the day of judgment than for you." And, "Tell them that the kingdom of God is at hand." And again, "It shall be recompensed to you at the resurrection of the just." Now, if the mention of these events (I mean, the judgment-day, and the kingdom

of God, and the resurrection) has a plain and absolute sense, so that nothing about them can be pressed into an allegory, neither should those statements be forced into parables which describe the arrangement, and the process, and the experience of the kingdom of God, and of the judgment, and of the resurrection. On the contrary, things which are destined for the body should be carefully understood in a bodily sense,—not in a spiritual sense, as having nothing figurative in their nature. This is the reason why we have laid it down as a preliminary consideration, that the bodily substance both of the soul and of the flesh is liable to the recompense, which will have to be awarded in return for the co-operation of the two natures, that so the corporeality of the soul may not exclude the bodily nature of the flesh by suggesting a recourse to figurative descriptions, since both of them must needs be regarded as destined to take part in the kingdom, and the judgment, and the resurrection.

(*On the Resurrection* 33)

So, again, the very reclining at the feast in the kingdom of God, and sitting on Christ's thrones, and standing at last on His right hand and His left, and eating of the tree of life: what are all these but most certain proofs of a bodily appointment and destination?   (*On the Resurrection* 35)

From these quotations it is evident Tertullian knew nothing of an abstract Kingdom. Tertullian conceived of the Kingdom in spatial terms.

4. Origen and Eusebius

Origen (ca. 185–254), the celebrated theologian of Alexandria[8] and Caesarea, wrote from a philosophical standpoint that was essentially Platonic and Stoic.[9] It is easy to understand, therefore, that although Origen conceived of the Kingdom as future,[10] nonetheless there is the tendency for

---

[8]The teacher of Origen was Clement of Alexandria. In preparation for this study I read G. W. Butterworth's *Clement of Alexandria* (Cambridge: Harvard University Press, 1919), which contains the text and translation of several of Clement's works. Clement's conception of the Kingdom as a future hope can be seen in his *Exhortation to the Greeks*, ch. 9; *The Rich Man's Salvation*, chs. 2, 3, 31, 32, and 42.

[9]The Origen quotations that follow are from A. Cleveland Coxe, ed., *Tertullian, Part Fourth; Minucius Felix, Commodian; Origen, Parts First and Second*, vol. 4 of *The Ante-Nicene Fathers*, cited above, n. 4.

[10]*De principiis* II.3.7, II.10.3; *Against Celsus* III.47, V.19.

him to portray the Kingdom as "spiritual" in nature.[11] But *indirectly* he is witness to the existence in the early Church of a sensory-spatial understanding of the Kingdom of God. Origen criticized those who do not understand that such statements as "Henceforth I shall not drink of this cup, until I drink it with you new in my father's Kingdom" should be taken *figuratively*. The following quotation from *De principiis* is intriguing and is cited in full.

> Certain persons, then, refusing the labour of thinking, and adopting a superficial view of the letter of the law, and yielding rather in some measure to the indulgence of their own desires and lusts, being disciples of the letter alone, are of opinion that the fulfillment of the promises of the future are to be looked for in bodily pleasure and luxury; and therefore they especially desire to have again, after the resurrection, such bodily structures as may never be without the power of eating, and drinking, and performing all the functions of flesh and blood, not following the opinion of the Apostle Paul regarding the resurrection of a spiritual body. And consequently, they say, that after the resurrection there will be marriages, and begetting of children, imagining to themselves that the earthly city of Jerusalem is to be rebuilt, its foundations laid in precious stones, and its walls constructed of jasper, and its battlements of crystal; that it is to have a wall composed of many precious stones, as jasper, and sapphire, and chalcedony, and emerald, and sardonyx, and onyx, and chrysolite, and chrysophrase, and jacinth, and amethyst. Moreover, they think that the natives of other countries are to be given them as the ministers of their pleasures, whom they are to employ either as tillers of the field or builders of the walls, and by whom their ruined and fallen city is again to be raised up; and they think that they are to receive the wealth of the nations to live on, and that they will have control over their riches; that even the camels of Midian and Kedar will come, and bring to them gold, and incense, and precious stones. And these views they think to establish on the authority of the prophets by those promises which are written regarding Jerusalem; and by those passages also where it is said, that they who serve the Lord shall eat and drink, but that sinners shall hunger and thirst; that the righteous shall be joyful, but that sorrow shall possess the wicked. And from the New Testament also they quote the saying of the

---

[11]E.g., in *De principiis* II.11.3, Origen agrees that in the Kingdom people will eat, but their food will be the "bread of life" that nourishes the soul with "the food of truth and wisdom."

Savior, in which He makes a promise to His disciples concerning the joy of wine, saying, "Henceforth I shall not drink of this cup, until I drink it with you new in My Father's kingdom." They add, moreover, that declaration, in which the Savior calls those blessed who now hunger and thirst, promising them that they shall be satisfied; and many other scriptural illustrations are adduced by them, the meaning of which they do not perceive is to be taken figuratively. Then, again, agreeably to the form of things in this life, and according to the gradations of the dignities or ranks in this world, or the greatness of their powers, they think they are to be kings and princes, like those earthly monarchs who now exist; chiefly, as it appears, on account of that expression in the Gospel: "Have thou power over five cities." And to speak shortly, according to the manner of things in this life in all similar matters, do they desire the fulfillment of all things looked for in the promises, *viz.*, that what now is should exist again. Such are the views of those who, while believing in Christ, understand the divine Scriptures in a sort of Jewish sense, drawing from them nothing worthy of divine promises.

(*De principiis* II.11.2)

There are three passages from *The Ecclesiastical History* (*Historia ecclesiastica*) by Eusebius of Caesarea that deserve notice.[12] The portrayal of the *basileia* as a future hope[13] can be seen in the winsome account of the appearance of the grandsons of Judas (the brother of Jesus) before Domitian.

> The same Domitian gave orders for the execution of those of the family of David and an ancient story goes that some heretics accused the grandsons of Judas (who is said to have been the brother, according to the flesh, of the Savior) saying that they were of the family of David and related to the Christ himself. Hegesippus relates this exactly as follows. "Now there still survived of the family of the Lord grandsons of Judas, who was said to have been his brother according to the flesh, and they were delated as being of the family of David. These the officer brought to Domitian Caesar, for, like Herod he was afraid of the coming of the Christ. He asked

---

[12]The Eusebius quotation that follow are from Kirsopp Lake, *Eusebius, The Ecclesiastical History,* vol. 1 (Cambridge: Harvard University Press, 1926).

[13]F. Edward Cranz, "Kingdom and Polity in Eusebius of Caesarea," *Harvard Theological Review* 65 (January 1952): 47-66. Cranz pointed out in this article that in the thought of Eusebius the destiny of man is the Kingdom of Heaven, and this destiny is to be realized when Christ comes again.

them if they were of the house of David and they admitted it. Then he asked them how much property they had, or how much money they controlled, and they said that all they possessed was nine thousand denarii between them, the half belonging to each, and they stated that they did not possess this in money but that it was the valuation of only thirty-nine plethra of ground on which they paid taxes and lived on it by their own work." They then showed him their hands, adducing as testimony of their labour the hardness of their bodies, and the tough skin which had been embossed on their hands from their incessant work. They were asked concerning the Christ and his kingdom, its nature, origin, and time of appearance, and explained that it was neither of the world nor earthly, but heavenly and angelic, and it would be at the end of the world, when he would come in glory to judge the living and the dead and to reward every man according to his deeds. At this Domitian did not condemn them at all, but despised them as simple folk, released them, and decreed an end to the persecution against the church.

(*Ecclesiastical History* III.19.1–20:5)

Though unfortunate, it is not surprising that in some segments of the Church the concept of a sensory Kingdom was given sensual overtones. If the testimony of Eusebius (quoting Gaius) is trustworthy, this perversion was true of Cerinthus. Though Cerinthus's conception of the Kingdom is invalid, nevertheless there must have been in the original tradition a sensory concept of the *basileia* that served as a basis for his perversion.

We have received the tradition that at the time under discussion Cerinthus found another heresy. Gaius, whose words I have quoted before, in the inquiry attributed to him writes as follows about Cerinthus. "Moreover, Cerinthus, who through revelations attributed to the writing of a great apostle, lyingly introduces portents to us as though shown him by angels, and says that *after the resurrection the kingdom of Christ will be on earth* and that humanity living in Jerusalem will again be the slave of lust and pleasure. He is the enemy of the scripture of God and in his desire to deceive says that the marriage feast will last a thousand years." Dionysius, too, who held the bishopric of the diocese of Alexandria in our time, in the second book of his Promises makes some remarks about the Apocalypse of John as though from ancient tradition and refers to the same Cerinthus in these words, "Cerinthus too, who founded the Cerinthian heresy named after him, wished to attach a name worthy of credit to his own invention, for the doctrine of his teaching was this, that the kingdom of Christ would be on earth, and being fond of his body and very carnal he dreamt of a future according to his own desires, given up to the indulgence of the flesh, that is, eating and drinking and marrying, and to those things which seem a euphemism for these things, feasts and sacrifices and the slaughter of victims.

(Ecclesiastical History III.28.1-5)

The third quotation from Eusebius embodies his discussion of Papias, "a man of very little intelligence, as is clear from his books."

The same writer adduces other accounts, as though they came to him from unwritten tradition, and some strange parables and teachings of the Savior, and some other more mythical accounts. *Among them he says that there will be a millennium after the resurrection of the dead, when the kingdom of Christ will be set up in material form on this earth.* I suppose that he got these notions by a perverse reading of the apostolic accounts, not realizing that they had spoken mystically and symbolically. For he was a man of very little intelligence, as is clear from his books. But he is responsible for the fact that so many Christian writers after him held the same opinion, relying on his antiquity, for instance Irenaeus and whoever else appears to have held the same views.

(Ecclesiastical History III.39.11-13)

From the preceding study of patristic literature[14] two conclusions concerning the Kingdom of God are obvious. First of all, in patristic literature (as in the Synoptics) the Kingdom was conceived as a *future hope*. The early Church Fathers knew nothing of a "realized" Kingdom. Secondly, the Kingdom was presented by the Church Fathers as a spatial phenomenon.[15] Some of them conceived of the Kingdom in strictly mundane categories, for example, Irenaeus, while others conceived of it in more "spiritual" terms, for example, Origen. Yet for all the Kingdom was a

---

[14]See Hans Bietenhard, "The Millennial Hope in the Early Church," *Scottish Journal of Theology* 6 (March 1953): 12-30, for the citation of additional patristic literature that reveals how the Church Fathers conceived of the Kingdom as a future hope.

[15]The initial turning from a concrete to an abstract understanding of the Kingdom probably took place in Alexandria under Clement and Origen. Note Origen's interpretation of Luke 17:21 cited by T. W. Manson on p. 595 of *The Mission and Message of Jesus* (New York: E. P. Dutton and Company, 1938). Christian thought, however, has been dominated by the Augustinian equation of the Kingdom with the Church. An abstract understanding of the Kingdom did not become a prominent feature of Christian thought until the nineteenth century.

Golden Age, a Coming Good Time to be experienced in the future by the people of God.

The conception of the Kingdom as both a place and a future hope dominated Christian thought until the time of Augustine. Augustine's contribution was the identification of the Kingdom with the Church.[16] C. H. Dodd argued that the *differentia* of Jesus' teaching concerning the Kingdom was that the *basileia* was in effect during Jesus' ministry. His thesis is contrary to the overwhelming bulk of synoptic data and to the understanding of the Kingdom held by the Church Fathers who were in proximity to the original tradition. Supporters of Dodd's hypothesis cannot evade this question: If Jesus proclaimed a Kingdom inaugurated in his ministry, why did the apostolic and the postapostolic Church misunderstand his proclamation? I believe they did not misunderstand Jesus. Jesus proclaimed the *imminence* of a *spatial* Kingdom. Because of this proclamation, the early followers of Jesus expectantly awaited its arrival.

---

[16]Louis Berkhof pointed out Augustine's identification of the Kingdom with the Church in his *The Kingdom of God* (Grand Rapids: Eerdmans, 1951). Berkhof's book is a lucid survey of the various concepts of the Kingdom of God that have prevailed throughout the history of Christian thought. Attention should also be called to Henry Martyn Herrick's *The Kingdom of God in the Writings of the Fathers* (Chicago: The University of Chicago Press, 1903). This is a helpful (though incomplete) guide to the concept of the Kingdom in patristic literature.

Bibliography

Argyle, A. W. "Does Realized Eschatology Make Sense?" *Hibbert Journal* 51 (July 1953): 385-87.

_____. "The New Testament Interpretation of the Death of Our Lord." *The Expository Times* 40 (June 1949): 253-56.

Bacon, Benjamin W. *Studies in Matthew*. New York: Henry Holt, 1930.

Barrett, C. K. "New Testament Eschatology." *Scottish Journal of Theology* 6 (September 1953): 136-55.

_____. "Q: A Re-Examination." *Expository Times* 54 (September 1943): 320-23.

Bellinzoni, Arthur J., editor. *The Two-Source Hypothesis: A Critical Appraisal*. Macon GA: Mercer University Press, 1985.

Bietenhard, Hans. "The Millennial Hope in the Early Church." *Scottish Journal of Theology* 6 (March 1953): 12-30.

Black, Matthew. "The Kingdom of God Has Come." *Expository Times* 63 (June 1952): 289-90.

Boismard, M.-E. "The Two-Source Theory at an Impasse." *New Testament Studies* 26 (October 1979): 1-17.

Borg, Marcus. *Conflict, Holiness and Politics in the Teaching of Jesus*. New York: Edwin Mellen Press, 1984.

Buchanan, George Wesley. *The Consequences of the Covenant*. Leiden: E. J. Brill, 1970.

_____. *Jesus: The King and His Kingdom*. Macon GA: Mercer University Press, 1984.

Bultmann, Rudolf. *History of the Synoptic Tradition*. Translated by John Marsh. New York: Harper & Row, 1963.

_____. *Theology of the New Testament*. Volume 1. Translated by Kendrick Grobel. New York: Charles Scribners, 1951; London: SCM Press, 1952.

Burrows, Millar. "Thy Kingdom Come." *Journal of Biblical Literature* 74 (March 1955): 1-8.

Buse, S. Ivor. "Spatial Imagery in New Testament Teaching About the Kingdom of God." *Expository Times* 60 (December 1948): 82.

Butler, B. C. *The Originality of St. Matthew: A Critique of the Two-Document Hypothesis*. London: Cambridge University Press, 1951.

Butler, Dom Christopher. "Three Books on the New Testament." *Downside Review* 65 (October 1947): 334-52.
Butterworth, G. W. *Clement of Alexandria.* Cambridge: Harvard University Press, 1919.
Cadbury, Henry J. *The Peril of Modernizing Jesus.* New York: Macmillan, 1937.
Cadoux, A. T. *The Parables of Jesus.* London: James Clarke & Co., 1931.
Cadoux, Cecil John. *The Historic Mission of Jesus.* London: Lutterworth Press, 1941.
_____. *Life of Jesus.* West Drayton: Penguin Books, 1948.
Campbell, J. Y. "The Kingdom of God Has Come." *Expository Times* 48 (December 1952): 91-94.
Chapman, Dom John. *Matthew, Mark and Luke: A Study in the Order and Interrelation of the Synoptic Gospels.* London: Longmans, Green and Co., 1937.
Clark, Kenneth W. "Realized Eschatology." *Journal of Biblical Literature* (September, 1940): 367-83.
Clavier, Henri. "The Kingdom of God: Its Coming and Man's Entry in It." *Expository Times* 60 (June 1949): 241-44.
Collingwood, R. G. *The Idea of History.* London and New York: Oxford University Press, 1946.
Conzelmann, Hans. *Jesus.* Philadelphia: Fortress Press, 1973.
_____. *The Theology of St. Luke.* Translated by G. Buswell. New York: Harper & Row, 1960.
Corley, Bruce, editor. *Colloquy on New Testament Studies: A Time for Reappraisal and Fresh Approaches.* Macon GA: Mercer University Press, 1983.
Cox, G. E. P. *The Gospel According to St. Matthew.* Oxford: Clarendon Press, 1945.
Craig, Clarence T. "Realized Eschatology." *Journal of Biblical Literature* (September 1940): 17-26.
Cranz, F. Edward. "Kingdom and Polity in Eusebius of Caesarea." *Harvard Theological Review* 65 (January 1952): 47-66.
Dalman, Gustaf. *The Words of Jesus.* Translated by D. M. Kay. Edinburgh: T.&T. Clark, 1902.
Danker, Frederick W. "Luke 16:16—An Opposition Logion." *Journal of Biblical Literature* 77 (September 1958): 231-43.
Dibelius, Martin. *Jesus.* Berlin: Walter de Gruyter, 1939.
Dodd, Charles Howard. *According to the Scriptures.* New York: Charles Scribner's Sons, 1953.
_____. *The Apostolic Preaching and its Developments.* London: Hodder & Stoughton, 1936; New York: Harper & Row, 1964.
_____. *The Bible and its Background.* London: Unwin, 1931, 1983.
_____. *The Bible Today.* Cambridge: Cambridge University Press, 1956.
_____. *The Coming of Christ.* Cambridge: Cambridge University Press, 1954.
_____. *Gospel and Law.* Cambridge: Cambridge University Press, 1951.
_____. *History and the Gospel.* London: James Nisbet & Co., 1938.

_____. *The Interpretation of the Fourth Gospel*. Cambridge: Cambridge University Press, 1953.

_____. "The Kingdom of God Has Come." *Expository Times* 48 (December 1936): 138-42.

_____. *The Parables of the Kingdom*. London: James Nisbnet & Co., ²1936 [¹1935, ³1936, ⁴1948, ʳᵉᵛ1961].

_____. "The Present Position of the Synoptic Problem." *Congregational Quarterly* 13 (April 1925): 206-12.

_____. "Present Tendencies in the Criticism of the Gospels." *Expository Times* 43 (February 1932): 246-51.

Douglas, Claude C. *Overstatement in the New Testament*. New York: Henry Holt, 1931.

Duncan, George S. *Jesus, Son of Man*. London: James Nisbet & Co., 1948.

Enslin, Morton Scott. *Christian Beginnings*. New York: Harper & Brothers, 1938.

_____. "Twixt the Dusk and the Daylight." *Journal of Biblical Literature* 75 (March 1956): 19-26.

Farmer, William R. *Jesus and the Gospel: Tradition, Scripture and Canon*. Philadelphia: Fortress Press, 1982.

_____, editor. *New Synoptic Studies: The Cambridge Gospel Conference and Beyond*. Macon GA: Mercer University Press, 1983.

_____. *The Synoptic Problem*. New York: MacMillan, 1964; corrected reprint: Dillsboro NC: Western North Carolina Press, 1976.

Farrer, A. M. "On Dispensing with Q." In *Studies in the Gospels. Essays in Memory of R. H. Lightfoot,* ed. Dennis E. Nineham, 55-58. Oxford: Basil Blackwell, 1957.

Filson, Floyd V. *One Lord One Faith*. Philadelphia: Westminster Press, 1943.

Flew, R. Newton. "Jesus and the Kingdom of God." *The Expository Times* 46 (February 1935): 214-18.

Foakes-Jackson, F. J., and Kirsopp Lake. *Prolegomena*. Volume 1 of *The Beginnings of Christianity,* 5 volumes. London: Macmillan, 1920.

Fuller, Reginald H. *The Mission and the Achievement of Jesus*. London: SCM Pess, 1954.

Gilkey, Langdon. *Message and Existence: An Introduction to Christian Theology*. New York: Winston-Seabury, 1979.

Gilmour, S. MacLean. *The Gospel Jesus Preached*. Philadelphia: Westminster Press, 1959.

Goguel, Maurice. *The Life of Jesus*. Translated by Olive Wyon. London: George Allen & Unwin Ltd., 1953.

Goulder, D. M. "On Putting Q to the Test." *New Testament Studies* 24 (January 1978): 218-34.

Grant, Frederick C. *Form-Criticism—A New Method of New Testament Research*. Chicago: University of Chicago Press, 1934.

Grant, Michael. *Jesus: An Historian's Review of the Gospels*. New York: Charles Scribner's Sons, 1973.

Guignebert, Charles. *Jesus*. Translated by S. H. Hooke. New York: University Books, 1956.

Harvey, Van A. *The Historian and the Believer*. New York: Macmillan, 1969.

Hawkins, John C. *Horae synopticae: Contributions to the Study of the Synoptic Problem.* Oxford: Clarendon Press, 1909.

Herrick, Henry Martyn. *The Kingdom of God in the Writings of the Fathers.* Chicago: The University of Chicago Press, 1903.

Hiers, Richard. *Jesus and the Future.* Atlanta: John Knox, 1981.

_____. *The Kingdom of God in the Synoptic Tradition.* Gainesville: University of Florida Press, 1970.

Hooker, Morna D. "New Testament Scholarship: Its Significance and Abiding Worth." *Bulletin of the John Rylands Library* 63 (Spring 1981): 419-36.

Hostetler, Marion Stewart. "The Place of B. H. Streeter in the Study of the Synoptic Problem." Ph.D. dissertation, The Hartford Seminary Foundation, 1952.

Howard, W. F. "The Best Books on the Kingdom of God." *The Expository Times* 48 (June 1937): 393-96.

Hunter, Archibald M. *Introducing New Testament Theology.* Philadelphia: Westminster Press, 1957.

_____. *The Work and Words of Jesus.* Philadelphia: Westminster Press, 1950.

Huston, Hollis. "The Q Parties at Oxford." *The Journal of Bible and Religion* 25 (April 1957): 123-28.

Hutton, W. R. "The Kingdom of God Has Come." *Expository Times* 64 (December 1952): 89-91.

Jeremias, Joachim. *Jesus' Promise to the Nations.* Translated by S. H. Hooke. Naperville IL: Alec R. Allenson, 1958.

_____. *The Parables of Jesus.* Translated by S. H. Hooke. New York: Charles Scribner's Sons, 1955.

Kee, Howard Clark, and Franklin W. Young. *Understanding the New Testament.* Englewood Cliffs: Prentice Hall, 1957.

Kittel, Gerhard. "The This-Worldly Kingdom of God in Our Lord's Teaching." *Theology* 14 (May 1927): 260-62.

Knox, W. L. *The Sources of the Synoptic Gospels.* Cambridge: Cambridge University, 1957.

Küng, Hans. *On Being a Christian.* New York: Doubleday, 1976.

Lake, Kirsopp. *Eusebius, The Ecclesiastical History.* Volume 1. Cambridge: Harvard University Press, 1926.

Laymon, Charles M. *The Life and Teachings of Jesus.* New York: Abingdon Press, 1955.

Lightfoot, J. B. *The Apostolic Fathers.* Volume 2. Cambridge: Harvard University Press, 1913.

_____. *History and Interpretation in the Gospels.* London: Hodder & Stoughton, 1935.

Loisy, Alfred. *The Origins of the New Testament.* Translated by L. P. Jacks. New York: MacMillan, 1950.

Lowe, Malcolm. "The Demise of Arguments from Order to Markan Priority." *Novum Testamentum* 24 (January, 1982): 27-36.

Lummis, E. W. "A Case Against Q." *Hibbert Journal* 24 (July 1926): 755-65.

_____. *How Luke Was Written*. Cambridge: Cambridge University Press, 1915.

Major, H. D. A., T. W. Manson, and C. J. Wright. *The Mission and Message of Jesus*. New York: E. P. Dutton, 1938.

Mann, C. S. *Mark: A New Translation with Introduction and Commentary*. Garden City NY: Doubleday, 1986.

Manson, William. *Christ's View of the Kingdom of God*. London: James Clarke and Co., 1928.

McCasland, Vernon. *By the Finger of God*. New York: Macmillan, 1951.

McCown, C. C. *The Search for the Real Jesus*. New York: Charles Scribner's Sons, 1940.

_____. "Symbolic Interpretation." *Journal of Biblical Literature* 63 (December 1944): 329-38.

McKnight, Edgar V. *What is Form Criticism?* Philadelphia: Fortress Press, 1969.

M'Neile, Alan Hugh. *The Gospel According to St. Matthew*. London: Macmillan, 1952.

Michael, J. Hugh. "A Conjecture on Matthew 11:12." *Journal of Biblical Literature* 77 (September 1958): 375-76.

Minear, Paul S. "Time and the Kingdom." *The Journal of Religion* 24 (April 1944): 77-88.

Moffat, James. *An Introduction to the Literature of the New Testament;*. Edinburgh: T.&T. Clark, 1918.

Nineham, D. E., editor. *Studies in the Gospels*. Oxford: Basil Blackwell, 1957.

Otto, Rudolf. *The Kingdom of God and the Son of Man*. Translated by Floyd V. Filson and Bertram Lee-Woolf. London: Lutterworth Press, 1943.

Parker, Pierson. *The Gospel Before Mark*. Chicago: University of Chicago Press, 1953.

_____. "A Second Look at the Gospel Before Mark." *Journal of Biblical Literature* 100 (1981): 389-413.

Perrin, Norman. *What is Redaction Criticism?* Philadelphia: Fortress Press, 1969.

Piper, Otto A. "The Mystery of the Kingdom of God." *Interpretation* 1 (April, 1947): 183-200.

Radford, J. Grange. "The Kingdom of God." *Expository Times* 46 *(June 1935)* 427-28.

Rawlinson, A. E. J. "The Kingdom of God in the Apostolic Age." *Theology* 14 (May 1927): 262-66.

Redlich, E. Basil. *Form Criticism—Its Value and Limitations*. London: Duckworth, 1939.

Reumann, John. *Jesus in the Church's Gospels: Modern Scholarship and the Earliest Sources*. Philadelphia: Fortress Press, 1969.

Richardson, Alan. "Kingdom of God" in *A Theological Wordbook of the Bible*. New York: Macmillan, 1950.

_____. *The Miracle-Stories of the Gospels*. London: SCM Press, 1941.

Roberts, T. A. *History and Christian Apologetic*. London: S.P.C.K., 1960.

Robinson, Theodore H. *The Gospel of Matthew*. New York: Harper & Bros., 1927.

Rowley, H. H. *The Relevance of Apocalyptic*. New York: Harper & Bros., 1946.

Scott, E. F. "The Place of Apocalyptical Conceptions in the Mind of Jesus." *Journal of Biblical Literature* 41 (June 1922): 137-42.

Schweitzer, Albert. *The Mystery of the Kingdom of God.* Translated by Walter Lowrie. New York: Macmillan, 1950.

Selby, Donald Joseph. "Changing Ideas in New Testament Eschatology." *Harvard Theological Review* 50 (January, 1957): 21-36.

Sharman, Henry Burton. *The Teaching of Jesus About the Future.* Chicago: University of Chicago Press, 1909.

Smith, B. T. D. *The Parables of the Synoptic Gospels.* Cambridge: Cambridge University Press, 1937.

Smith, Harold. "The Kingdom of God in the Ante-Nicene Fathers." *The Expository Times* 30 (March 1919): 248-50.

Stoldt, Hans-Herbert. *History and Criticism of the Marcan Hypothesis.* Translated and edited by Donald Niewyck and introduced by William R. Farmer. Macon GA: Mercer University Press, 1980.

Stonehouse, N. B. *The Witness of Luke to Christ.* London: Tyndale Press, 1951.

Taylor, Vincent. "The Elusive Q." *Expository Times* 46 (November 1934): 68-74.

_____ . *Jesus and His Sacrifice.* London: Macmillan, 1937.

_____ . "The Order of Q." *The Journal of Theological Studies* 4 (April 1953): 27-35.

Von Dobschütz, Ernst. *The Eschatology of the Gospels.* London: Hodder and Stoughton, 1910.

Walker, William O., Jr., editor. *The Relationships Among the Gospels: An Interdisciplinary Dialogue.* San Antonio: Trinity University Press, 1978.

Weiss, Johannes. *Jesus' Proclamation of the Kingdom of God.* Translated by Richard Hiers and David Holland. Philadelphia: Fortress Press, 1971.

Werner, Martin. *The Formation of Christian Dogma.* Translated by S. G. F. Brandon. London: Adam & Charles Black, 1957.

Wilder, Amos N. *Eschatology and Ethics in the Teaching of Jesus.* New York: Harper & Bros, 1950.

Wilson, William E. "The Kingdom of God in This World." *Anglican Theological Review* 28 (October 1946): 181-91.

Indexes

1. Scripture References

Psalms
2:7 109
110:1 109

Isaiah
6:9-10 .... 88, 109
35:5-6 84
42:1-4 77
61:1-2 84

Matthew
3:1-2 .... 17, 53, 55, 122
3:8 125
3:10-17 89
3:11 124
3:19 .... 73, 123
3:24-30 .... 54, 93, 123, 125
3:31-33 .... 79, 123
4:8 .... 48, 125
4:17-18 .... 58, 84, 119
4:23 .... 73, 122
5:3 124
5:10 124
5:14-16 32
5:19-20 .... 17, 18, 51, 53, 121, 122
5:39-40 27-28
6:10 .... ii, 10, 17, 81, 119
6:23 125
6:31-33 .... 54, 124
7:21-23 .... 18, 53, 55, 84, 122
7:28-29 70
8:3 68
8:10-13 57
8:11 .... 10, 50, 53, 60, 120
9:2-8 71
9:18 68
9:29 68
10:1 70
10:5-8 .... 58-59, 119
11:2-6 .... 46, 65-66, 83
11:11-13 .... 10, 66, 91, 121, 124
11:16-19 90
12:13 46
12:18-21 .... 77, 78
12:25 .... 48, 125
10:27 .... 74, 80
10:28 .... ii, viii, 5, 10, 39,
    46, 65, 67, 71, 73-77, 81-82, 119
12:41-42 .... 46, 66, 89
13:8 125
13:10-17 89
13:11 124
13:16-17 .... 46, 66, 87
13:19 .... 73, 123
13:24-30 .... 54, 93, 123, 125
13:31-33 .... 79, 123
13:36-45 .... 17, 53-54, 57, 123
13:49-50 .... 17, 57, 93
13:52 .... 52, 124
14:25 40
16:19 124
16:28 .... 54, 58, 119, 121
18:1-4 .... 52, 121-22
18:3 53
18:4 18
18:23-35 .... 17, 123
19:12 .... 52, 124
19:14 .... 52, 124
19:23-25 .... 17, 53, 55, 122
19:28-29 .... 52, 55
20:1 124
20:20-34 .... 51, 68
20:21 121
21:31 .... 52-53, 122

21:43 124
22:1-14 51
22:2 124
23:13 .... 53, 122
24:7 .... 48, 125
24:14 .... 73, 122
25:1-12 .... 56, 124
25:34 .... 17, 119
26:27-29 .... 50, 58, 120

Mark
1:14-15 .... 46, 65-66, 85, 119
1:22 70
1:31 68
1:41 68
2:18-20 .... 42, 56
3:5 68
3:10 68
3:15 70
3:24 48
3:27 10
3:28-30 71
4:11 .... 6, 124
4:26 124
4:30-31 124
5:23 68
5:25-34 68
5:41 68
6:2 68
6:7 70
6:14 69
6:23 48
6:56 68
7:32-33 68
8:22 68
8:25 68
9:1 .... 54, 58, 119, 121
9:47-48 .... 17, 53, 57, 122
10:13 68
10:15 .... 53, 125
10:23-25 .... 17, 53, 122
10:26 55
10:35-40 17
11:10 119
11:27-33 70
12:13 70
12:34 125
13:8 48
14:25 .... 10, 50, 60, 120
15:43 .... 54, 120
21:43 17

Luke
1:35 71
3:28-29 10
4:11-12 88

4:14 72
4:32-36 .... 69, 70
4:40 68
4:43 73
5:13 68
5:17 .... 69, 73
6:17-19 68-69
6:20-23 .... 55, 125
6:29 .... 27, 28
7:20 51
7:22-23 .... 10, 65
7:28 121
8:1 73
8:10 .... 88, 125
8:46 68
8:54 68
9:1-2 .... 17, 59, 70, 73
9:11 73
9:27 .... 10, 54, 58, 120-21
9:60 73
9:62 125
10:9 120
10:11 120
10:19 70
10:21-22 87
10:23-24 .... 10, 66, 87
10:25-28 87
11:2 .... ii, viii, 10,
            65, 67, 74-77, 81-82, 120
11:10 17
11:13 68
11:17 48
11:20 .... ii, viii, 10,
            65, 67, 74-77, 81-82, 120
11:31-33 .... 32, 66, 89
12:5 71
12:31-34 .... 17, 54-55, 125
13:2-28 57
13:18-19 124
13:20-21 124
13:22-29 .... 55-56, 60, 120
13:28 .... 53-54, 121
13:43 17
13:52 19
14:15 .... 17, 50, 120
14:16-24 51
15:43 17
16:16 .... 5, 66, 73, 86, 91
16:17-18 126
16:28 17
17:20 10
17:21 .... viii, 5, 17, 53, 125
18:4 10
18:16-17 .... 53, 122, 125
18:23-26 .... 17, 53, 55, 83, 122

8:29-30 .... 55, 125
19:11 .... 17, 120
19:12 .... 10, 126
19:15 126
20:20-23 10
21:10 .... 48, 126
21:29 33
21:31 .... 18, 120
22:14-16 .... 18, 50, 58
22:17-18 .... 10, 17, 121
22:28-30 .... 17, 50, 121
22:51 68
23:42 120
23:50-52 .... 17, 54, 120
24:49 72

John
3:3 127
3:5 127
18:36 127

Acts
1:3 127
1:6 127
2:16 102
2:22 68
4:7 70
8:12 127
10:36-38 .... 72, 79
14:22 127
19:8 127
20:25 127
28:23 127
28:31 127

Romans
11:7-8 88
14:17 127

1 Corinthians
1:24 69
4:20 127
6:9-10 127
6:14 69
15:24 127
15:50 127

2 Corinthians
5:17 102
13:4 69

Galatians
5:21 127

Ephesians
5:5 127

Colossians
1:13 127
4:11 127

1 Thessalonians
2:16 82
2:12 127

2 Thessalonians
1:5 127

2 Timothy
4:1 127
4:18 127

Titus
3:5 102

Hebrews
1:8 127
11:33 127
12:28 127

James
2:5 127

1 Peter
1:23 102

2 Peter
1:11 127

1 John
2:8 102

Revelation
1:6 127
1:9 127
5:10 127
11:15 127
12:10 127
17:12 127
17-17-28 127

2. Names and Subjects

Argyle, A. W., 103, 113, 114
Augustine, 21, 59, 62, 77, 140
Bacon, Benjamin W., 87, 88, 90
Barrett, C. K., 9, 25, 27, 36, 103
Beelzebub, 74
Beelzebul, 74, 78, 81
Bellinzoni, Arthur J., 20
Bietenhard, Hans, 139
Black, Matthew, 85
Boismard, M.-E., 19
Book of Discipline, 10
Borg, Marcus, 75, 76
Bousset, Wilhelm, 14
Bowman, John Wick, 102
Buchanan, George Wesley, 61
Bultmann Rudolf, 3, 22, 29, 61, 63, 68, 80
Burrows, Millar, 61, 80, 81, ii
Buse, S. Ivor, 60
Butler, B. C., 17, 19, 20, 22, 24
Butterworth, G. W., 135

Cadbury, Henry, 35, 115
Cadoux, A. T., 94
Cadoux, Cecil John, 7, 8, 38
Campbell, J. Y., 85, 86
Cerinthus, 138
Chapman, Dom John, 25
Clark, Kenneth W., 79, 80, 85
Clavier, Henri, 60
Clement of Alexandria, 21, 59, 128, 129, 135
Collingwood, R. G., 109, 110, 111
Common Catechism, 10
Consistent Eschatology
  how advanced by Johannes Weiss, 3-4
  how combined with realized eschatology, 9-10
  how produces theological, Christological, and professional problems, 62-64

Conzelmann, Hans, 31, 93
Corley, Bruce, 20
Cox, G. E. P., 75
Coxe, A. Cleveland, 133
Craig, Clarence T., 85, 103
Cranz, F. Edward, 137

Dalman, Gustaf, 38, 61, 97, 98
Danker, Frederick W., 91
DeArmey, Dr. Michael, ix
Dibelius, Martin, 3, 61, 64, 83
Didache, 131
Dodd, C. H.
  his attitude toward Albert Schweitzer, 8
  his attitude toward Mark and Q, 14-18
  his ambiguous use of "kingdom," 38-48
  his philosophy of history, 103-106
Domitian, 137
Douglas, Claude C., 82
Duncan, George S., 7

Enlightenment, 1
Enslin, Morton Scott, 3, 7, 22, 29, 61
Epistle of Barnabus, 131
Eusebius of Caesarea, 127, 137

Farmer, Willam R., 19, 34
Farrer, Austin, 20, 24, 29, 33
Filson, Floyd V., 7, 97
Fiorenza, Elisabeth Schüssler, 102
Flew, R. Newton, 7
Foakes-Jackson, F. J., 26
Fuchs, A., 19
Fuller, Reginald H., 10, 85

Gaius, 138
Gilkey, Langdon, 9, 10, 60
Gilmour, Maclean, 7
Goguel, Maurice, 61

Goulder, D. M., 23
Grant, Frederick C., 29, 49, 61
Grant, Michael, 63
Grant, R. M., 61
Guignebert, Charles, 3, 7, 49, 61
Haddan, Arthur West, 77
Harnack, Adolf von, 62
Harvard Divinity School, 117
Harvey, Van A., 14
Hauer, Dr. Stanley, ix
Hawkins, Sir John, 14
Hendrick, Charles B., 49
Herrick, Henry Martyn, 140
Hiers, Richard Hyde, 2, 9, 61, 62, 63, 102
Holland, David Larrimore, 2, 62, 63
Holtzmann, Heinrich Julius, 20
Hooker, Morna D., 5
Hostetler, Marion, 25, 27, 36
Howard, W. F., 5
Hunter, Archibald M., 6, 7
Huston, Hollis, 29
Hutton, W. R., 85

Irenaeus, 59, 132, 139

Jenni, Ernst, 102
Jeremias, Joachim, 61, 94
Jesus
  his healing ministry, 67-73
  his Kingdom proclamation, 48-60
  summary of his Kingdom proclamation, 58-59
John the Baptist, 86
Jonah-Solomon, 90
Joseph of Arimathea, 54
Judas (brother of Jesus), 137
Judas of Galilee, 92

Kaftan, Julius, 3, 63
Kee, Howard Clark, 7
Kingdom of God
  its centrality in Jesus' teaching, 2
  its multiple meanings in *Parables of the Kingdom*, 38-48
  its meaning in the Synoptics, 48-60
  patristic literature concerning, 127-140
  listing of all references to Kingdom in Synoptics, 119-126
  parables concerning, 92-96
  how diversely interpreted in Christian thought, vii
  as understood by mediating theologians, 9-10
  as understood by consistent eschatologists, 61-62
  as summary of Jesus' teachings, 58-59
Kittel, Gerhard, 5
Knox, W. L., 24

Küng, Hans, 63, 64
Lake, Kirsopp, 26, 137
Laymon, Charles M., 7
Lee-Woolf, Bertram, 97
Lessing, G. E., 1
Lightfoot, R. H., 31
Loisy, Alfred, 3, 61
Lummis, F. W., 24, 35
MacMullen, R. G., 77
Major, H. D. A., 90
Manson, T. W., 28, 90, 139
Manson, William, 5
Marcan Priority
  pivotal role in *Parables of the Kingdom*, 13-18
  dethroning of Marcan Priority theory, 19-23
Marsh, John, 80
McCasland, S. Vernon, 67, 68, 79
McCown, C. C., 13, 103
McKnight, Edgar V., 29
McSwain, Eunice, ix
Mediating theologians, 9, 46, 48
Michael, J. Hugh, 91
Miller, Dr. Samuel, 117
Minear, Paul S., 7
M'Neile, Alan Hugh, 89, 90, 91
Moffat, James 27
Moore, George Foot, 61

Nineham, D. E., 24, 31

Oesterreich, T. K., 79
Old Cambridge Baptist Church, 117
Origen, 21, 135, 139
Otto, Rudolf, 5, 97, 98
Outler, Albert C., 33, 34
Oxford Society of Historical Theology, 102

Papias, 132
Parable of the Fishnet, 93, 94
Parable of the Weeds, 93
Parker, Pierson, 20, 22, 23
Pentecost, 44, 72
Perrin, Norman, 31
Piper, Otto A., 7
Polycarp, 59, 130, 132
Q, 14, 15, 16, 17, 18, 19, 23, 24, 27
  dethroning of Q hypothesis, 23-28
  document or stratum, 35-36
  pivotal role in *Parables of the Kingdom*, 13-18
Radford, J. Grange, 60
Rauschenbusch, Walter, 62
Rawlinson, A. E. J., 60, 127
Realized Eschatology
  its wide acceptance in New Testament studies, 5-7
  as an alternative to consistent eschatology, 7-8

how combined with consistent eschatology, 9-10
two versions of realized eschatology—"Kingdom" and "Christological," viii
how first presented in *The Parables of the Kingdom,* 4
Realized Eschatology (Christological version)
  content of, 101-112
  evaluation of, 109-112, 115-118
Realized Eschatology (Kingdom version)
  evaluation of, 96, 114-115
  content of, 65-96
  six crucial synoptic passages supporting, 65-66, 74-92
  synoptic parables, 92-96
  not supported by Rudolf Otto and Gustaf Dalman, 97-99
Redlich, E. Basil, 29
Reimarus, Herman Samuel, 1, 2
Reumann, John, 2
Richardson, Alan, 7, 72
Rist, Martin, 102
Roberts, Harold, 7
Roberts, T. A., 31, 109, 110, 112
Robinson, Theodore H., 89, 90
Rowley, H. H., 8
Schaff, Philip, 77
Schussler, E., 102
Schweitzer, Albert, 3, 8, 46, 47, 49, 61, 64, 101, 115
Scott, E. F., 5
Selby, Donald Joseph, 82
Sharman, Henry Burton, 4, 5

Smith, B. T. D., 94
Smith, Harold, 5
Southern Baptist Theological Seminary, viii
Stendahl, Krister, 3, 75, 85
Stoldt, Hans-Herbert, 19, 20, 21, 23
Stonehouse, N. B., 75
Streeter, B. H., 14, 19, 29
Taylor, Vincent, 7, 9, 25, 27
Tertullian, 59, 133
Tillich, Paul, 118
Tobias, 80
Troeltsch, Ernst, 118
Two-Document Hypothesis, viii, 11
  its pivotal role in *The Parables of the Kingdom,* 13-18
  dethroning of Two-Document Hypothesis, 19-35
  as a methodological error in *The Parables of the Kingdom,* 30-35
United Methodist Church, 10
Ur-Marcus, 22
von Dobschütz, Ernst, 60
von Harnack, Adolf, 62
Weiss, Johannes, 2, 48, 49, 62, 64, 101, 115
Werner, Martin, 61
Wilder, Amos, 61
Williams, Joan, ix
Wilson, Willam E., 7
Wisdom Christology, 91
Woods, F. H., 22
Wright, C. J., 90
Young, Franklin W., 7